CORK
FOOTBALL

with Denis Hurley

PUBLISHED BY HERO BOOKS
LUCAN
CO. DUBLIN
IRELAND

Hero Books is an imprint of Umbrella Publishing
First Published 2023

ISBN: 9781910827444

A CIP record for this book is available from the British Library

Cover design and formatting: jessica@viitaladesign.com
Photographs: Sportsfile

★ DEDICATION ★

To the Cork football person, possessed of durable spirit
and incurable dedication

And to my late, great friend James Milner…
I know we're beating Kerry wherever you are

★ CONTENTS ★

★ ACKNOWLEDGEMENTS ★

IF YOU EVER happen to come across footage of the 1990 All-Ireland football final on YouTube, you might be able to make out a red and white crepe hat right at the front of Hill 16, dead centre behind the goal. It's perched on the head of a six-year-old me, not realising how lucky I was.

Lucky first of all to be brought to the game – and the hurling final a fortnight previously – by my father, Jim and lucky to be enjoying a time when Cork were at the pinnacle of Gaelic football. The double was followed by Arsenal winning the English league title the following spring, and it was only when Cork City were denied the League of Ireland title in a last-day shootout against Dundalk that I realised that my teams didn't always win.

That was hammered home in further trips to All-Ireland football finals with my father – 1993 against Derry, and 1999 against Meath, when a bid for another double just fell short. By 2007 and the hammering against Kerry, I was travelling on my own steam (though 'steamed' might be a more appropriate word for me, and my school and college friends making the journey).

A few weeks after that loss, I was taking my first steps in journalism and by the time of Cork's next final appearance in 2009, again against Kerry, I was working. I wasn't in the press box, though – over-subscription there meant I was sitting next to *Echo* columnist, Joe Kavanagh as we struggled to stay composed as Cork moved into an early 1-3 lead. The restraint was a shrewd move, as Kerry came back to inflict more heartbreak.

Thankfully, in 2010, Cork managed to go all the way, defeating Down in the final. By this stage, I had come to know many of the squad through work. I was live-blogging the game for the GAA's official website – I've never gone back to see if the last few entries were any way coherent – and a few tears were spilled as Graham Canty lifted the Sam Maguire Cup.

CORK FOOTBALL IS subject to two unflattering sources of comparison: on the one side is Kerry, the standard-bearers of Gaelic football, with more All-Ireland wins than anyone else, and on the other is Cork hurling, currently between spells on top of that roll of honour.

For the football faithful on Leeside, there is a dichotomy of hope and fatalism… 'Do you know something, we might actually give the All-Ireland a rattle this year, but knowing us, we won't even make the Munster final'. Certainly, nobody could accuse Cork of ever having success come easy – usually, it only follows after a heart-breaking struggle. And, then, when they do sometimes make it to the top, the refrain is that, however much silverware has been claimed, they should have won more.

The 25 players whose stories feature in this book enjoyed some measure of joy in a Cork jersey, but none was without some disappointment. To their credit, none of them ducked any questions about the bad days and it makes for a deeper understanding of their journeys. The words inside are theirs: all I had to do was transcribe them. If it were possible, I am more privileged than I was at six – my job allows me the perfect cover for peppering with questions those who made me star-struck.

To Liam Hayes of Hero Books, who entrusted me with writing Larry Tompkins' autobiography, *Believe*, in 2020, and then the hurling equivalent of this book, I cannot express enough thanks, especially given his patience with the floating deadline technique I employed. Liam also deserves credit for not excising the constant mentions from the members of the 1990 panel about Cork beating Meath; he says he has 87 or 88 reasons for not doing that, but I'm unsure what he means.

I'm ever thankful to my bosses, *The Echo* sports editor, John McHale and his deputy, Eamonn Murphy for allowing me a work environment that allows me to eventually finish a project like this. Barry O'Mahony and Jack McKay are new additions to the sports desk and, hopefully, we will all covering major Cork football successes again before too long.

To my friends, within sports journalism and beyond: assistance was not explicitly sought but it was a comfort to know it was there. In no order – and apologising for any forgetful exclusions – I have benefited from the counsel and company of Niall O'Flynn, Gary Carroll, Tommy Canavan, Fintan O'Toole,

Paul Dollery, Eoghan Cormican, John Coleman, Lisa Lawlor, John Roycroft, Mary White, Robert O'Shea, Kieran McCarthy, Tracey Kennedy, Joe Blake and Finbarr McCarthy.

Of course, like football, life is not without its challenges. My mother, Gretta did as much as anyone to foster a love of language and literature, but she will never read this or any of my books due to the unfairness of the onset of dementia at far too young an age. I know that she would be proud and, hopefully, she still feels the love that we all have for her.

Something like that brings a family together. I can't emphasise enough my admiration for my siblings, Susan, Lorna and James in taking things in their stride, helped of course by their own spouses, Cathal, Joe and Ruth respectively. A squad of grandchildren is developing nicely too and, hopefully, my father, Jim can escort them to big days in Croke Park, just like he brought me long ago.

In Peter and Frances Lynch, my 'outlaws', I couldn't have wished for a better set of second parents. The assistance, advice and love provided is something I can never repay. My siblings-in-law, Conor and Katie, and their partners, Jen and Seán, are all incredibly dear to me and I'm proud to be part of such a tight unit.

To my sons, Johnny and Aaron – whatever path life takes you on, may you be filled with the same kind of resilience as Cork football displays. Like Conor Counihan said after the 2010 win, know that failure is merely the fuel for success.

And to Jess, my wife – I love you more than I did yesterday and I'll love you more tomorrow.

Denis Hurley
August 2023

CON 'PADDY' O'SULLIVAN
(& BILLY MORGAN)

CORK 2-7 ★ KERRY 1-7
Munster SFC Final
Fitzgerald Stadium
JULY 17, 1966

★ **CORK: B Morgan**; B Murphy, J Lucey, T O'Leary; J O'Sullivan, F Cogan, J Crowley; M Burke (0-1), M O'Loughlin; E Philpott (0-1), G McCarthy (1-1), F Hayes; E Ryan (0-3), **C O'Sullivan (0-1)**, J Carroll (1-0). **Subs:** J O'Mahony for O'Leary, K Dillon for O'Sullivan, N Fitzgerald for O'Loughlin.

★ **KERRY:** J Culloty; Donie O'Sullivan, P O'Donoghue, M Morris; Denis O'Sullivan, JD O'Connor, T O'Callaghan; M O'Connell (0-1), M Fleming; P Moynihan (0-2), S Fitzgerald, D O'Shea; T Prendergast (0-2), P Griffin (0-1), PJ Fitzpatrick (0-1). **Sub:** T Barrett (1-0) for Fitzpatrick.

66

I STARTED OFF with Cork in May 1956.

I cycled about 12 miles in the morning to Castletownbere to get a spin up to Cork. We were playing Kerry in the final of the Gaelic Week Tournament and the man that was on me was Mick O'Connell – it was his first day out for Kerry, too.

I had never played minor for Cork. Beara were fielding hardly any minor teams at the time. Some of the good players, like Paddy Harrington – father of Pádraig, the golfer – or Riobard O'Dwyer were going to school in Rochestown College and they would have actually played minor with St Finbarr's inside in the city.

In the first round of the senior championship in 1956, we played Millstreet in Bantry. They were the defending champions and I was playing on 'Toots' Kelleher that day and he would have been the *man* in Cork at the time. We lost by two points but I had a good game on him – the Kerry match was a week later and I was

THE ACTION

★★★★★

THE WIN IN Killarney ended a 10-year wait for a triumph over the Kingdom. In the first-half, there seemed to be little sign that Kerry's gallop to a ninth consecutive Munster crown would be stopped. They were sharper and took a 0-5 to 0-3 lead in with them at the interval.

On the restart, Gene McCarthy had a point for Cork from a free before Eamonn Ryan sent over an excellent shot to level. As Con 'Paddy' O'Sullivan made his presence felt around midfield alongside Mick Burke, Cork looked set to capitalise but couldn't make it count on the scoreboard. The failure to make the most of that period of dominance was punished as frees from PJ Fitzpatrick and O'Connell had Kerry in front again, but they proved to be their last points. After they were reduced to 14 players with the dismissal of Séamus Fitzgerald, Cork pushed on.

When wing-back Johnny Crowley made a driving run and then sent in a high ball, Johnny Carroll was there to win it and fire to the net. Cork had the lead for the first time and would not relinquish it. After a point from Burke, Cork struck for another goal, albeit one that materialised in fortuitous circumstances – having won the kickout, Gene McCarthy drove towards goal and shot for the top corner but the ball ricocheted off full-back Paud O'Donoghue, and flew past Johnny Culloty, leaving Cork five in front.

★★★★★

called up. The Gaelic Week Tournament was a competition run by Paddy Tyers, whose son Brian commentates on TG4 now – Paddy was also our goalkeeper!

I actually played two games that day – in the evening, Beara played Lees in the challenge match up at the Mardyke. Lees was a club set up by West Cork men who had moved to the city – they were three-quarters Beara as well! Back home after that, and cycled out to Urhan – it was three or four o'clock in the morning and the birds were signing. I slept that night, let me tell you!

Sometimes, for a match you left on Saturday and got a bus up to Cork and you wouldn't be coming back until Monday morning. It was tough going. When I moved to Cork, the logistics became a lot easier!

For a while, I was working in Whitegate and living in Cloyne, and I became friendly with Christy Ring. In 1958, there were three of us from Beara down there and we had to get back for a semi-final against Macroom in Bantry. We asked Christy for a lift but he was heading somewhere else. At the end of the field, he spotted a broken hurley and he took up the handle part of it. He said, 'Look, put that into the top of your bag and go up to the cross – I'll bet you that nobody will pass you!' We did and we were hardly there a couple of minutes before a man stopped, coming from Churchtown South. 'Are ye going hurling?' he asked, and so off we went, into Cork. That was the quick thinking of Ring!

I wasn't on the Cork championship panel in 1956 – they made it to the All-Ireland final, losing to Galway – but I was called up in 1957. I was a sub on the senior team up until the Munster final and I was playing for the juniors too. The seniors made it back to the All-Ireland final, though I wasn't involved, and they were beaten by Louth. The juniors got to the final too but we lost as well, against Mayo.

I played in all different positions. I never minded what jersey I got on the day. Centrefield was a lovely place to play, if you had a good spring in you at all. You'd have to be on your toes, ready to jump, because there were so many good fielders. There's nobody jumping now. The football was very robust back then. Macroom were strong and so were Clonakilty but apart from themselves and Beara, there was no other West Cork team.

Eamonn Young was in charge at the time. He was a tough man – he'd tell you whether you were playing well or badly, and you'd take it or leave it. After 1957, Cork didn't win Munster again for nearly a decade. It wasn't until Eamonn

Young came back again in 1966 that we beat Kerry – down in Killarney, against all the odds. It was frustrating losing to Kerry each year. In 1958, they came with a young team – Mick O'Dwyer, Mick O'Connell, Séamus Murphy, Tom Long, Kevin Coffey, Dave Geaney and a good friend of mine, Donie O'Sullivan – and they got a good 10 or 12 years out of those fellas. We found it very hard to beat them, but at the same time I never considered retiring.

Urhan won the junior in 1960 and we had to go senior, so I was away from Beara for a few years. The intermediate grade wasn't revived until 1965 so we regraded when that came back. Then in 1967, we won the double – Beara won the senior and Urhan won the intermediate. Divisional teams were allowed to take part in the Munster Club Championship at the time and Beara won that too!

Kilbride from Meath were Leinster club champions. We invited them down to Beara for a challenge match and they had plenty celebrations the night before, so we beat them easily enough. They were very fond of Smithwick's!

In May 1966, we went over to America for the Cardinal Cushing Games, kind of a precursor to the All Star tours. The highlight of that was being invited to The White House. We met Robert Kennedy – he used to come to Gaelic Park and throw in the ball – and I still have the photo.

There was a big Chinese community around Gaelic Park and they'd be hanging off the wire, anxious to see what was going on inside – but they never actually paid to get in. John 'Kerry' O'Donnell owned Gaelic Park and, being the cute Kerryman he was, he told the Cushing committee that, apart from Christy Ring, the one man he wanted out in New York was Jimmy Whan from Armagh. He put up a sign saying, 'Come and see the great Jimmy Whan play football!' and he got their money that way!

For the 1966 Munster final, it was a full house, though the exact figure is probably open to interpretation. People used to get in over the wire and everything. You couldn't count the crowd!

I was picked at full-forward, but one of our midfielders, Mick O'Loughlin, got injured midway through the game and I was moved out there on O'Connell. Often at full-forward I had been marked by Niall Sheehy – oh my God, he was a tough man, you can write it down – though that day it was Paud O'Donoghue.

Eamonn Young had us primed well for Kerry. He organised the whole thing and he picked the best players he could. He introduced long training runs where everyone was timed and ranked. This brought out a competitive streak in some of the lads who found they did not show up as well as they thought they should. He was a great presence in the dressing-room. He used to say to us, 'If I was dressed as a solider, I wouldn't think twice about shooting someone. Ye're dressed as soldiers going out on to the field… so be ready to shoot!'

Kerry had been ahead, but Johnny Carroll got a great goal for us and that put us in front. I did well on O'Connell. After the game, O'Connell would always shoot straight off the field, no hanging around. But that evening, we were in the Imperial Hotel in Killarney and he sent in Johnny Culloty to have me come out to meet him – he was in a car with Culloty, Mick O'Dwyer and Donie O'Sullivan. He congratulated me on winning a Munster Championship and wished me luck in the future. It was worth a gold medal to hear that from such a great player and I'll always remember it. The celebrations that night were brilliant. Eamonn Young, God rest him, he got up on a chair in the corner and sang *The Scottish Soldier*. That was his song; victory or defeat, he'd sing it. It's a lovely song.

After beating Kerry, we played the great Galway three in-a-row side in the All-Ireland semi-final. We had to wear the blue Munster jerseys, and they wore white. There was great football played that day. I was playing on Noel Tierney of Galway, a massive man, but I got a few points off him. I was fouled for a penalty that Denis Coughlan scored, but we lost by two points.

In 1967, we won Munster again; we beat Kerry down the Park and then beat Cavan in the semi-final. Unfortunately, we fell to Meath in the All-Ireland final. We were very close to them, but they got a lucky goal. I made piles of friends from all over, including Meath. When they won the All-Ireland, they had a trip to Australia and we were even fundraising for them – I sold tickets down here to send them to Australia! Any time they had an anniversary function, they invited us and myself and Denis Coughlan always travelled up. They kept us in the best hotels up there, there was never a problem.

I'd still keep in touch with the lads I played with for Cork; there's a very strong bond there. Of course, I'd like to have won an All-Ireland but It wasn't the most important thing. A lot of those medals rust. Friends are better than any medal.

★ ★ ★ ★ ★

BILLY MORGAN

66

I WASN'T ALWAYS a goalkeeper. I used to be out the field as a young fella and I played centre-forward with the Cork minors in 1963. We drew with Kerry in Killarney – we should have won – and then they won the replay and went on to win the All-Ireland.

After my minor year, I had an altercation with an official in Nemo and I went away playing soccer with Tramore Athletic for a year. They put me in goal, because I was a Gaelic footballer, I suppose. By the time I came back to football, I was in UCC and Dave Geaney, the manager of the Sigerson Cup team, needed a goalkeeper and approached me to see if I'd play there, and I did. I always thought that, when I came back to Nemo, I'd be out the field again but they kept me in goals – apart from the odd few games late in my career when they might have been stuck for numbers.

Maybe playing in goal in soccer was a bit more challenging because you had to control a bigger area, whereas in GAA you had to more or less stay on your line. It's all a lot different now – shot-stopping is only a smart part of the role.

I think I was good in the air. Soccer goalkeeping was way different to GAA in that you had to control your box – I loved coming for crosses, but that probably cost me in that first Munster final. A ball came into the square and the backs and forwards were jumping for it; I came out and jumped as well and a fella by the name of Tony Barrett got a fist to it and it went into the empty net.

I got on the Cork under-21 team in 1965 and we went to the All-Ireland final – we were beaten by Kildare in a great game. Cork seniors had been beaten by Limerick in the semi-final of the Munster Championship that year and it was seen as a new low. Eamonn Young and Donie O'Donovan came in to train the team and they changed a lot.

A load of the under-21s were brought into the panel. There was myself, Frank Cogan, Tim F Hayes and a few others. The training was very good and a new spirit developed. Brian Murphy from Crosshaven was the senior 'keeper and he played in the league of 1965-66 and I was the sub. We played Offaly in a challenge match in Tullamore on Easter Sunday of 1966 and I played in goal, that was my first game.

Brian played as a back with his club and, in training and practice matches when somebody might be missing, he was put in corner-back a lot. He ended up getting a place in the team at corner-back and I was delighted with that as we were very friendly. He was a genuine fella and he performed well there; he played corner-back for three or four years.

I didn't find the step up to be too difficult to deal with or anything. Obviously, you were playing against better standard of players but I was playing for UCC in the Sigerson and that was a very high standard. I can remember my first Sigerson, up in Belfast, and Seán O'Neill was playing for Queens. He had always played wing-forward up to then and it was the first time he was put full-forward and he was mesmerising – they got three goals, and he scored one and made the other two. From that point of view, you'd have trickier forwards at inter-county but I never felt it was beyond me.

There was no specialised goalkeeper training but I did a lot of work on my own. I went away and I bought Peter Shilton's book about the way he trained and the things he did, stuff you could do on your own. At the old Nemo, down at the end there was a stone wall and the surface was uneven – you'd kick the ball at the wall and it could come back at any angle, so I used that for my reflexes. There was another wall at The Farm in Bishopstown, where UCC trained, and I used that too. One day, a weasel shot out of that wall, something I hadn't been expecting! Jim Cremin, God rest him, used to play in goal on the Nemo hurling team and the two of us used to work together, too.

In my first year playing in goal, my kickouts were notably short. The full-back line was Brian Murphy, Jerry Lucey and Johnny O'Mahony and none of us had a huge kick, though Jerry wasn't too bad. One day, the issue was being discussed and Youngie said, 'I could piss farther than Billy Morgan!' When I was taking the kickouts, it would usually be a short one, so I could say I invented the short kickout – I had to, I had no choice! Jimmy Kerrigan used to say to me later on that, if I had been around at the same time as John Kerins, I'd never have been heard of! Kerinsie would set the ball down, take a step back and ping it 50 yards.

As time went on, they got better – I'd be quite honest, I worked hard at my kickouts. I used to go out to the '45' and try to put the ball over the bar from there. The day I eventually achieved it, the ball bounced off the crossbar and over!

I remember Johnny Carroll slagging me – I was well into my thirties at this stage – and he said, 'You're getting better at the kickouts'. When I was in America, there was a golf pro that used to be trying to coach us; he's always be saying to have a nice easy swing and follow-through and then develop that. So, I brought the same philosophy to football, not trying to kick as hard but making sure I had my head down and that I was following through.

In the first round of the 1966 championship, we played Clare up in Ennis and we beat them well. That put us into the Munster final against Kerry in Killarney and we beat them too, which was a first since 1956.

The first Munster final that I can remember attending was in the old Athletic Grounds in 1954, when Kerry beat Cork. Two years later, I was there when it was a draw, but I didn't go to Killarney for the replay that Cork won; the first time I was in Killarney for a game was when I was playing minor, in 1963.

We used to travel by hackney. Those getting the 'city car' used to meet at the old county board rooms at Cook St. Denis Coughlan used to get it, Frank, myself, Eric Philpott – that was generally our group. We'd usually leave at around 10am to give ourselves time and then meet at the Imperial Hotel in the middle of Killarney; it's now known as the Towers.

You'll be familiar with the ritual of the 'championship haircut'. Before the All-Ireland under-21 final, I got a haircut and we lost. I got a haircut before another big game soon after that and we lost that too, so I decided after that that there were to be no more trims in the lead-up to matches! It probably sounds stupid, really.

In fairness to Donie and Eamonn, when they came in, they improved the whole lot. Their training was brilliant. Youngie was probably known as the Christy Ring of football in Cork.

The under-21s were coming through and Cork underage football in general was strong at the time. They won the minor All-Ireland for the first time in 1961 and then in 1964 they should have won it again but they were beaten in the final by Offaly. There were young fellas coming in with a different mindset, and Donie and Youngie helped to strengthen that mindset.

After the Munster minor final in 1963, I remember staying on to watch the senior match and a young fella came on for Kerry, only just out of minor and he was outstanding – it was Pat Griffin. He later became a garda and his son, Pádraig won county titles with Clonakilty and played for Cork, though he tragically died in 2022.

In the 1966 final, Pat was soloing through and, all of a sudden, he was met with a clatter by one of our team! There was a bit of a melee but, in fairness to Pat, he wasn't all that angry. I suppose he felt the blood pouring from his nose spoke for itself! That's one thing I remember… and I made a good save in the second-half, too.

We led more or less all the way through. They had a man sent off in the second-half – Séamus Fitzgerald, who later played corner-back but was centre-forward that day. We were well ahead by that stage, but with the extra man we were never going to lose. Twenty-one years later, my first Munster title as a manager would also come in Killarney against a 14-man Kerry side!

In the semi-final in 1966, we were playing for Galway, who were going for their third All-Ireland in-a-row. They went on to achieve that, but they only beat us by two points. We had two great goal chances – they both fell to Niall Fitzgerald, a great player who was remembered for kicking the winning point in 1956.

Johnny Geraghty saved one, and the other went wide. Niall, who was a grand fella, a great footballer and a true servant to Cork football, had actually retired and was brought back in that year as a sub. He did well in Killarney and then he came in against Galway and was unlucky. He had been remembered for the point in 1956 but then he was remembered for missing those two chances, which was unfair on him.

I didn't think that it would take seven years for us to make the breakthrough and win the All-Ireland. We won Munster again in 1967, beat Kerry by a point on a wet day down the Park. We beat Cavan in the semi-final and we were very lucky to win that, but we should have beaten Meath in the final.

The score at half-time was 0-4 to 0-1… and it should have been about 0-10 to 0-1. We missed some awful chances. They had the wind in the second-half but we did well enough. They just got that goal, which was the difference in the end. They got a 14-yard free in front of the goal and Tony Brennan went for a point but miskicked the ball, and it came in low. Jerry Lucey caught it and belted it out the field and everybody ran out – except Meath's Terry Kearns. I remember, he was leaning on his knees by the post.

Mattie Kerrigan caught it and sent it back in. I knew Terry was where he was, but Denis Coughlan was coming back in and my initial instinct was to break it down to Denis. At the last minute, I decided to try to catch it, but Kearns' fist came up and glanced the ball over my shoulder and into the net. We lost by 1-9 to 0-9 and I often think about that one, even now.

We started the 1968 Munster final against Kerry like a house on fire. Donal Hunt and Ray Cummins were making their debuts that day and we were 2-1 to 0-0 after 10 minutes but then Mick O'Connell took over. He was outstanding. Kerry lost to Down in that year's All-Ireland final but they went all the way in 1969 and '70.

It was frustrating, knowing that we could beat them on our day but were never able to carry it on to the All-Ireland, whereas they could. I often felt that, such a big effort went into trying to get over Kerry – all the training and everything that went with it – that the next game was often an anti-climax. Like 1971, for example.

In the Munster final, we beat Kerry down the Park by 11 points, 0-25 to 0-14 – it was an 80-minute game. They were up by 0-10 to 0-6 at half-time but we came out for the second-half and we were brilliant; Kevin Jer O'Sullivan in particular I remember had a great game. We met Offaly then in the semi-final and we were flat. They beat us by five points after they got a last-minute goal, and they went on and won the All-Ireland.

In 1972, Kerry beat us again in Killarney. It was a very hot day and we were a youngish team whereas they still had their older players. Just after half-time, Donie Sheehan – a chemist from Killarney, who was involved in the Kerry County Board for years – was walking around behind the goal and he said, 'Ah Billy, ye have us, I think!' – typical Kerry plámas! They beat us by six or seven points.

Nemo won the Cork senior championship for the first time in 1972, under a fella called Dinny McDonnell. He pushed us to the limit in every aspect. Back then, the county champions would have the chairperson of the Cork selection committee and Dinny was Nemo's choice.

Donie O'Donovan had packed it in after 1968 – there was an issue between

Glen Rovers and the county board over a lifetime ban issued to a player, and the Glen and St Nick's withdrew all their selectors from Cork teams. In 1972, I was part of a group of players that went to Donie and asked him to come back and we were able to persuade him.

He was the trainer and Dinny McDonnell made a point of sitting beside Donie during matches – anything that he wanted done, Dinny would get it done. Dinny got in Dr Paddy Fitzgerald from UCC as the team doctor, and he asked Donie and Mick 'Langton' McCarthy from St Nick's about getting a masseur, something we had never had before. Langton found John 'Kid' Cronin, who stayed involved with Cork teams for the next two decades, until he died just after the 1993 All-Ireland football final.

It was much more professional set-up and right from day one, we felt confident. At this stage, the younger fellas were coming to the fore. The team that won the 1967 minor All-Ireland was one of the best to ever come out of Cork and you'd fellas coming through from that – Dinny Long, Ned Kirby, Kevin Kehilly. They were full of belief because they were only ever used to beating Kerry at minor and under-21 level, so there was an attitude about us all.

For three weeks coming up to a big match, I wouldn't touch a drink but then, the night beforehand, I'd have two pints. In 1966, before the All-Ireland semi-final, we stayed in the Lucan Spa and I went up to bed at around 10pm or half past, but I couldn't sleep. I was a bag of nerves. I went for a walk down around the foyer and I bumped into 'Weeshie' Murphy – Dr Con's father – who was county board chairperson at the time, and he was with Eamonn Young.

Eamonn asked what was wrong and when I said I couldn't sleep, Weeshie asked if I took a drink? I said I drank Guinness and he brought me into the bar...'Give that young fella a pint of Guinness!' I was chatting away with the lads and, when I was finished, he called another one for me. When I had that drunk, he told me to go away up to bed... and I slept soundly. After that, it became my ritual before games.

Before the 1973 final, we were staying in the Skylon Hotel in Drumcondra and a good few of us, maybe 10 of the team, went across to The Ivy House on the Saturday night. We had a pint each and called another round, but the glasses from the first round were still on the table – a few Cork supporters came in and couldn't believe what they were seeing!

We were confident for that final. The training had gone well and we were happy with our preparations and the match-ups. They had a young fella, Morgan Hughes, at corner-forward and he had been excellent in the championship but Frank Cogan went on him and he snuffed him out. Maurice Burke at right half-forward was another fella who had been very impressive, but Connie Hartnett went back to mark him and did a great job. Then you had Jimmy Barry, of course!

At half-time, we were four or five points up but Galway came back well at the start of the second-half and then they got a goal – one that would have repercussions in 1976. Tom Naughton took a shot and I pushed the ball on to the post and fell against it. As I was getting up, I turned around and the ball was on the line, so I picked it up… but the umpire raised the green flag. I protested and inside in the dressing-room afterwards, a reporter asked about that and I said, 'The ball was not over the line'. The following day, the *Irish Independent* had a picture of me up against the post and the ball clearly over the line!

The referee that day was John Moloney from Tipperary and he was in charge again, with the same umpires, when we played Kerry in the Munster final in the new Páirc Uí Chaoimh. That day in 1976, we were seven points up against Kerry and the umpire started talking to me. 'Remember '73, you were wrong about that?'

I said, 'I know, I was… but when I turned around I saw it on the line'.

Soon after that, Kerry had a chance that Brian Murphy caught on the line but the goal was given – and to my dying day, I'll swear that that one wasn't over the line. It had come from a free and the two umpires had gone behind the goal, thinking it would be tapped over the bar. Brian caught the ball, but the next thing the umpire was picking up the green flag. I ran over to protest but he said, 'You were wrong in '73… and you're wrong again now!' I couldn't say another word and Kerry beat us.

I didn't have any speech written before the 1973 final. I think it's a bit ridiculous sometimes, seeing fellas with foolscap pages, reading out a big, long speech. All you need to do is just the normal things – thank the selectors, thank the trainer, thank the supporters and commiserations to the beaten team. One extra thing I did say was to congratulate Tyrone, who had won the minor final beforehand – I mentioned the problems they were having up there. After the match, we were in the pub near the Skylon and a northern fella came up to me and said, 'Did ya mean what ya said, there?' I said I did, and he thanked me.

When I was in college, there were a few fellas I was friendly with who had Republican leanings. Later, Noel Dunne the Cork hurler told me that he had played golf one day with a fella who was in Special Branch. He was telling Noel which fellas they were watching… and I was one of those on the list after that speech!

After 1973, the celebrations were above and beyond up until Christmas. At that time, Donie said that it was time to get down to work, but the celebrations kept going. We went out to San Francisco in March 1974 for the All Star tour and Donie had to threaten us again. 'If ye're not going to knuckle down, I'm out of here.'

We beat Kerry in Killarney and beat them well, and we were fairly confident going up to play Dublin in the All-Ireland semi-final – over-confident, really. I can remember, we were about four points down with five minutes to go and I was thinking, *We have to be careful here or we're going to be beaten.* Dublin were a second-division team that year, but Kevin Heffernan had come in and raised fitness levels. Brian Mullins at the time was a PE teacher and Heffo made the most of that… they were super-fit. They ran us off the pitch.

We copped ourselves on then and the first league match of the 1974-75 season was against Dublin in Croke Park, and we beat them. Going to Killarney to play Kerry in 1975, we were confident again – going for a three in-a-row in Munster – but Mick O'Dwyer had picked up on what Dublin had done and Kerry had the legs on us. The team broke up after that.

Winning as a manager compared to winning as a player, it's different. Nothing beats playing. Coaching is only ever a substitute. One lesson that was learned was to avoid over-celebrating. When we won the All-Ireland in 1989 against Mayo, Mick O'Dwyer said that it was a Mickey Mouse final, and a couple of the Meath lads compared it to a practice match. We had won the All-Ireland without beating Meath, so there was a determination to put that right. The mindset was different, too – the 1989-90 team were good boys to celebrate, but at the right time. They would work very hard and train very hard and then, after a match, they'd let the hair down. To complete everything, we had to beat Meath in the championship and we did.

JOHN COLEMAN

CORK 3-17 ★ GALWAY 2-13
All-Ireland SFC Final
Croke Park
SEPTEMBER 23, 1973

★ **CORK:** B Morgan; F Cogan, H Kelleher, B Murphy; K O'Sullivan, **J Coleman**, C Hartnett; D Long (0-3), D Coughlan (0-1); N Kirby (0-1), D Barron (0-1), D McCarthy; J Barry-Murphy (2-1), R Cummins (0-8), J Barrett (1-2). **Subs:** S Coughlan for Coleman, D Hunt for McCarthy.

★ **GALWAY:** G Mitchell; J Waldron, J Cosgrove, B Colleran; L O'Neill, TJ Gilmore (0-1), J Hughes (1-0); W Joyce, J Duggan (0-2); M Burke (0-2), L Sammon (0-1), M Rooney; J Coughlan, T Naughton (1-0), M Hughes (0-7). **Subs:** F Canavan for Coughlan, C McDonagh for Burke.

66

ON THE THIRD Sunday of September, 1967, Cork were due to play Laois in the All-Ireland minor football final. Two dual players – Séamus Looney and Simon Murphy – had both been injured playing in the minor hurling final and would miss the football.

So, there was a trial game fixed for the Monday night before the final to find replacements; it was against the Cork seniors, who were playing Meath in the All Ireland senior final and I was called in for the match, even though I was still quite young for minor. I had just returned to school at Rockwell College in Tipperary, but my father collected me and brought me to the Mardyke for the game. I was selected at left half-forward and happened to be marking the great Frank Cogan – I somehow got a goal and four points the same night, and it always intrigued me afterwards how he let me off with it.

THE ACTION

★★★★★

THE REBELS ONLY trailed for about 90 seconds, right at the start of the match, following the opening score from a Morgan Hughes free. Cork took the lead when Jimmy Barry-Murphy punched to the net after Jimmy Barrett's free had come back off the post, and they would hold the advantage from there until the end.

Ray Cummins, Cork's free-taker, was in splendid form in that first-half. In defence, John Coleman Denis Coughlan and Brian Murphy were extremely solid, and at half-time it was 1-10 to 0-6 for Donie O'Donovan's side.

At the start of the second-half, however, Galway began to show more purpose as they set about eating into the lead. Cork were made of stern stuff though – two fine frees, one from each sideline by Denis Long and Cummins ensuring that they remained well in control. Any time that Galway came back at them, Cork responded, and with the Munster champions defending so well, the goal that Galway needed was not looking like coming.

It did arrive though, in lucky circumstances as Tom Naughton's shot squirted over the line. It meant that Cork's lead was cut to four points, 1-14 to 1-10, but two more Cummins frees – he would finish with eight points – settled them before the signature moment of that match.

It was the 19-year-old Barry-Murphy who provided it, showing the impudence of youth as he took a pass from Cummins and dummied a solo before firing to the net.

★★★★★

When we became teammates later, I asked him why he didn't 'put the halters' on me that night and his reply was, 'I'd never do that to a young fellow – anyway, I was sure of my place for the final!' A true reflection of the man.

There was a minor selector at the time known as Donal 'Beag' O'Sullivan, or 'Small Donal', from Beara. He was a teacher in Douglas and he came onto the field after the match, told me I was in with a right shout for the final and asked me for my details. The minute I gave my date of birth, he said, 'Oh dear, you're only 16… that may come against you'.

Anyway, he informed me that the team would be on *The Cork Examiner* on Wednesday morning, and I couldn't wait to see the paper. First thing on Wednesday, I took off from Rockwell through the fields to the village of New Inn a mile away… into the shop and bought the paper. One sports column heading read, **'Two changes on Cork minor team'**… my heart was pounding and I thought, *Maybe this is it…* but I couldn't see the name anywhere. I counted out the numbers – 21, the correct number; the starting 15 plus six subs. Out of luck… Donal Beag was right.

I went back to the college through the fields, very disappointed, but to add to the misery, I had missed maths class as a result and so I was sent to the Dean of Discipline's office and got six across the arse with the strap for my troubles. I sat on the marble stairs to cool off, fairly despondent, and was only a stone's throw from thumbing it home there and then.

When I went down for lunch that day there was a letter from Donal Beag, who had taken the trouble to write to me, encouraging me and telling me not to be disappointed as I had lots of time on my side. A wonderful gesture from a pure gentleman. By the weekend, I had got permission to go to Croke Park with my father, who picked me up in Rockwell on the Sunday morning. We had tickets for the Canal End, standing in the corner watching the Cork minors absolutely trounce Laois. As things transpired, had I been on the panel for that final, I would have ended up with three consecutive All-Ireland minor football medals, something that hasn't been done since. Brian 'Beano' McDonald of Laois won two in 1996 and '97 and reached a third minor final in '98 – the same day as our 1973 team were honoured as the silver jubilee team – but a late goal for Tyrone denied him the three in-a-row.

I had been to Croke Park on a few occasions with my father, even for All-

Irelands that Cork weren't involved in, but 1968 was my first time playing there. We had beaten Kerry in the Munster final and Dublin in the All-Ireland semi-final, and then beat Sligo in the final. In 1969, we retained the title by beating Galway in the semi-final and a Derry team in the final that included Martin O'Neill, the future Irish soccer manager.

Millstreet were fairly strong at underage when I was growing up – Connie Hartnett and myself collected five Duhallow divisional minor championship medals in-a-row. This was all down to one man, a wonderful teacher we had in the national school at that time, Bill O'Keeffe, who absolutely lived for Gaelic football. He had a great way about him and he brought so many players through the underage system in Millstreet with his unique coaching style that we all bought into. An amazing man.

I was called into the Cork under-21 team in my last year at minor and was lucky enough to play for four years in that grade, winning two more All-Irelands, beating Fermanagh in the 1970 and '71 finals. Actually, the only time I ever captained a Cork team was my last year at under-21 level in 1972 – there was no county under-21 championship at the time so they gave the captaincy to the longest-serving player – but we lost to Kerry in the Munster final in Killarney by a point; the only time we had lost to Kerry in six years under age. So be it.

My brother, Billy and I were sent to secondary school in Rockwell College where rugby was a religion. I played out-half and was lucky enough to win a Munster Schools' Junior Cup medal in 1967, beating Mungret in the final at Thomond Park. When I returned home that summer for the holidays, I bumped into the secretary of Millstreet GAA Club who happened to be pumping his tyres at our family's garage. He greeted me with, 'The very man – I need to reinstate you!'

I didn't know what 'reinstate' meant at the time but had I known it, I wouldn't have agreed to sign anything. When the form was sent to the county board, I was suspended for three months – May, June and July… for playing college rugby! My father was livid as I missed the whole summer of football with Millstreet. When he was dropping me back to the college in September, he told me, 'No more rugby now, sure they wouldn't know the shape of a rugby ball around Millstreet, so why are you bothering with it?' I knew immediately that this was easier said than done!

Halfway down the long hall in Rockwell was the notice board with the list of players for the first training session for the senior rugby team. I was on the list, but I never showed up; I hadn't the bottle to tell the priest. That evening as I was going into the refectory for tea, I got a tap on the shoulder. 'Where the hell were you today?'

I sheepishly replied, 'I'm not playing anymore rugby, Father because of the "foreign games ban",' and I knew straightaway that this was a big problem. The turbulence encountered for the next four weeks was a time I'll never forget, but I couldn't budge for my father's sake. One particular coach, who trained me to win an East Munster medal in the pole-vault, took particular offence. But a Tipp man saved my bacon.

He was Séamus Leahy, one of the famous Leahy family of Tipp hurling, who taught me English. He called me over one day after class. He mentioned that he heard that I was getting grief from the rugby people and suggested that I come away hurling with his side for the year. Rockwell hadn't won a hurling trophy for over 40 years. I told him I had never played hurling, but he said he'd sort that.

The team had two lads from Golden, Liam O'Sullivan and Liam Harding, who were on the Tipp minor panel, and Séamus built a strong team around them. In the final of the Corn Phádraig, the Munster B championship, we beat Templemore CBS in Thurles. I did enjoy the hurling and will always be grateful for Séamus Leahys's support. However, I really missed the rugby as everything in Rockwell revolved around it.

But the stance we took opened the way to secure a first of five All-Irelands medals in six years.

I first came into the Cork senior team in 1970, for a league match in Salthill against Galway – playing right corner-forward and marked by Noel Colleran, Enda's brother. He was a tough cookie and it was a real welcome to senior football for a young fellow. I never minded playing different positions, though I always felt I was on the small side for centre-back; compared to someone like Tommy Joe Gilmore from Galway, who was a horse of a man!

The first time I played centre-back was the 1971 senior All-Ireland semi-final against Offaly, which we lost by five points. Things improved after that – we started getting fed properly! We were playing a league match in Tralee that November and I remember, the famous 'Toots' Kelleher, another Millstreet man, was driving us that day. We beat Kerry by a point and afterwards were invited in for a meal of steaks. We learned for the first time that Kerry were being fed for years like this. With us, it was a case of going to Paddy Crowley's pub off Oliver Plunkett St or the Courthouse Tavern after training for a bottle of orange and a sandwich.

Kevin 'Jer' O'Sullivan had enough of it after that, and he decided he wouldn't go to training until we were fed like the Kerry boys. A few more went out in sympathy with him. Billy Morgan rang me one day at work – by this stage, I was involved in the family garage business selling tractors and cars in Millstreet. He said that we needed to get it sorted and a meeting was arranged with county board officers. At the time, the county board offices were in Cook St and we met them at the old Victoria Hotel just around the corner.

The chairman at the time was 'Big' Donal O'Sullivan – to distinguish him from our minor selector from the late 1960s. He was another proud Beara man, like Kevin Jer. He kicked off the meeting by asking, 'Kevin Jer, what's it going to take to get you back playing football for Cork?'

Kevin Jer's reply… 'Prawns and steak!'

The meeting almost ended there and then but, thank God, common sense prevailed. From the following week we were fed properly in the Victoria Hotel after training and matches. It's amazing to think we were All Ireland champions in a year and a half – it was the only time I recall being thankful to Kerry in relation to football!

Also in 1971, 'the Ban' was lifted and I got a phone call from a fellow that had been in Rockwell with me; he was involved with Highfield in Cork. Millstreet and Cork had been knocked out of the championships and he said to come away up for the winter.

I said I'd go along, as a way of keeping fit more than anything else, but the minute I touched the ball I knew I had missed it. I played junior the following week and senior a week after that. I was playing out-half and I was enjoying every minute of it. I got a Munster trial but I didn't make the team that year, but I did the following year.

My weekly winter schedule was to train Monday night with Millstreet, Tuesday with Highfield, Wednesday with Munster at the Army barracks in

Fermoy, Thursday with Cork at the Athletic Grounds… and Friday off. A rugby match on Saturday and a football match Sunday. I did that for three years but then I tore a cartilage the third year and I took the surgeon's advice that, 'A robot would have difficulty in doing what you were doing'. Anyway, it was becoming increasingly difficult to serve two masters.

Still, I had a great innings, winning 12 Munster caps at inside centre and playing on the team beaten by the All Blacks in 1974 in Thomand Park. The following January, I played in the first 'B' international, against France in Lansdowne Road. I recall the great rugby journalist, Ned van Esbeck of *The Irish Times* ringing me from time to time – I was easily contactable because of the business! And he'd say, 'Would you not give up the football for a couple of seasons and give the rugby a proper go?'

I recall answering him, 'Jesus Ned, you don't understand – down here it's all football'.

In the early 1970s, for games at the Athletic Grounds, we used to tog out in the Showgrounds. For the 1973 Munster final, Donie O'Donovan had a masterplan to try and derail the Kingdom. Kerry always played Paudie O'Donoghue at full-back marking Ray Cummins and, just before we went out on the pitch, Donie called everyone together and said, 'The minute the ball is thrown in, Ray is going to the corner and Jimmy Barry is switching to full-forward'.

Something like that wouldn't even be remarked on nowadays, but it was incredible how it upset the Kerry defence. Paudie didn't know what to do – he was shouting to the bench, asking if he should follow Ray or stay where he was? He stayed at full-back, the plan worked like a dream and Jimmy Barry created chance after chance, and we had five goals scored before half-time. Kerry were at sixes and sevens… we won by 5-12 to 1-15.

I was one of four Millstreet men on the team that year. Humphey Kelleher was full-back, I was centre-back, Connie Hartnett was left half-back and Dinny Long midfield. Din Connors from the town had been left half-back on the previous Cork team to win the All-Ireland, in 1945, and he was a relation of Connie's. All the time I was playing with Connie, there was only one jersey he would ever wear and that was No 7. If the No. 7 jersey was missing, he'd wear a blank. Talk about superstition!

Other Millstreet teammates, Fr Jim Kennelly, his brother, Ted, Tommy

Kelleher and Tommy Burke, were on the extended Cork panel at that time and, even though they didn't make the squad for the All-Ireland final, it was an amazing achievement for the club. We did have a smashing senior side at the time and in the lead-up to the All-Ireland final, Donie O'Donovan asked for a challenge game between the club and the full Cork side – the four of us played the first-half with Cork, and the second-half with Millstreet, who lost in a close encounter in the Athletic Grounds. A real proud day for the club. Unfortunately, we were beaten by a star-studded Carbery side in a quarter-final replay in Macroom in August 1973; it was a game we really should have won the first day.

In the All-Ireland semi-final, we were due to play Tyrone. I got married to Mary Buckley in August of that year and we were only back from the honeymoon just in time for the match. We drove around France; I had done my own training over there. The grain fields in France don't have many ditches so we'd pull in the car and I'd do laps of the cornfields with a ball. Mary didn't mind at all, thankfully!

We had said to the travel agent, 'Whatever you do, have a bed on the boat on the Friday night returning from Liverpool to Dublin'. But when we went to check in, there was no booking for us… so we slept in Pullman chairs that night.

Thankfully, we beat Tyrone to advance to the final against Galway. Because the game was being shown on television, the red against maroon was considered a colour-clash and Cork lost the toss and would have to wear white. Typical of the attention to detail of Donie O'Donovan, he wanted us to train in white jerseys as part of our preparation and Tyrone sent down their set, with the big red hand on the front. It was a nice touch by them and it was a great help.

I had been at the 1957 final with my father. Toots Kelleher was playing that day and he got injured – my father and himself would have been great friends, so we went to the dressing – room under the Cusack to see how he was? I can recall Toots togged out next to a pillar. Every time I went to Croke Park after that, I togged out in the same place as Toots.

The day of the final I was third or fourth into the dressing-room and here was this fella sitting in my spot, with his arms folded. It was Dermot O'Brien, captain of the Louth team that had beaten Cork in 1957.

'I came in to wish ye luck because we robbed ye in '57 and ye deserve to go all the way this time'. It was a lovely gesture from a true sportsman.

Galway had beaten Offaly in their semi-final and their star man was centre-forward and captain, Liam Sammon, who was outstanding. Donie told me, 'Whatever about playing your own game, you have to make sure that Sammon is curtailed, he is the difference in that Galway forward line'. For the weeks before it, I tried to make sure in training that whoever was on the '40' wasn't getting any ball.

In the final, I went off with a head injury late on and ended up having to go to the Mater Hospital with Kevin Jer O'Sullivan and Dinny Long. Gene Fitzgerald was a TD for Cork Mid at the time. He would go on to become Minister for Finance in the Haughey government but he was also treasurer of the county board. He asked us how we were getting to the Mater and we said we'd get a taxi, but he threw us the keys of his car – a very generous thing to do.

All three of us left the hospital together and went straight to the Green Isle Hotel on the Naas Road for the reception for the team, being held by the Corkmen's Association. When we arrived at the front door, we realised we had no tickets.

We tried to explain to the doorman that we were with the party inside but he was having none of it. Then who should arrive but Jack Lynch and he congratulated us before going in – the embarrassed doorman couldn't open the door wide enough for us!

Even though we had won, I wasn't overly pleased with my own performance, getting injured and everything. We were over in Leopardstown the following day at the reception for the two teams and a replay of the match was being shown. I was only half-watching it but, a couple of minutes after I had gone off injured, Sammon got a ball and rounded Declan Barron – who had been moved back to centre-back – and sent it over the bar. Michael O'Hehir said, 'His first score of the game'… and that phrase eased the burden somewhat and perked me up. On the following Tuesday night, the team brought the cup to Millstreet and what an amazing night was had.

Still, there is always a feeling out there that that was a talented Cork team that should probably have won more.

We won Munster again in 1974, and one of the backroom team went to watch the Leinster final between Dublin and Meath. He reported back to the management and players at Monday night's training session, and his first words were, 'Well now lads, I wouldn't lose any sleep over Dublin'. It was precisely the wrong thing to say and it proved a real momentum-changer; the edge evaporated from our training and complacency set in. When that happens, it's nearly impossible to eradicate it. Dublin beat us and went on to comfortably beat Galway in the final.

The other great 'What if?' was the 1976 Munster final replay against Kerry in the new Páirc Uí Chaoimh, when they were awarded a dubious goal and we were denied one immediately after at the other end – a six-point swing that was to prove too much for us.

The referee that day, John Moloney, used to referee hurling games when I was in Rockwell and I never had an issue with him. When we were leaving the stadium after that game, John was leaving at the same time. I said to him, 'Jesus John, whatever about the first goal, how could you disallow Barron's goal?'

It was obviously the umpire's decision; these guys officiated with him at games the whole year round, in wind and rain and snow all over the country, and he obviously had difficulty in over-ruling them. He was a very genuine bloke and afterwards was very regretful about the whole thing. I know it was just a game, but it was a tough pill to swallow.

I retired from inter-county at 29, but continued playing with the club until 1992, after winning back the Duhallow Junior football title. So, at the ripe old age of 42, I called it a day... but it left me with great memories shared with some amazing characters.

We've since had two memorable 50th anniversary reunions, one in Páirc Uí Chaoimh and one at Croke Park on All-Ireland final weekend, and I must acknowledge and sincerely thank Cork County Board and its officers, who went to great extremes to make it all such a memorable occasion for those of us lucky enough to be still around.

Unfortunately, Teddy O'Brien, Séamus Coughlan, Humphrey Kelleher and Connie Hartnett have gone to their eternal reward, but we'll never forget them.

Ar dheis Dé go raibh a n-anamacha.

99

TADHG MURPHY
(& JOHN CLEARY)

CORK 3-10 ★ **KERRY 3-9**
Munster SFC Final
Páirc Uí Chaoimh
JULY 17, 1983

★ **CORK:** M Creedon; M Healy, K Kehilly, J Evans; M Hannon, C Ryan, J Kerrigan; D Creedon, C Corrigan; **T Murphy (2-2)**, E O'Mahony, D Barry; D Allen (0-2), J Allen, **J Cleary (1-6)**. **Subs:** T O'Reilly for Barry, E Fitzgerald for O'Mahony.

★ **KERRY:** C Nelligan; G O'Keeffe, J O'Keeffe, P Lynch; P O'Shea, T Kennelly, M Spillane; J O'Shea (2-0), V O'Connor; G Power (0-1), D Moran, T Doyle; M Sheehy (0-7), E Liston, J Egan (0-1). **Subs:** JL McElligott for J O'Keeffe, S Walsh (1-0) for Power.

66

BACK IN 1983, I used to work on South Mall and we'd often go to the Long Valley pub for our lunch – they used to do a very substantial corned beef salad sandwich. Coming up to the Munster final that year, Mrs Moynihan behind the bar insisted on giving me two sandwiches for the entire week – she wanted me ready for Kerry!

In 1974, Cork won the two minor All-Ireland finals and I was on both of those teams – Johnny Crowley from Bishopstown was on the two teams as well. Also, that year, I was captain of St Finbarr's College – better known as Farranferris – and we won the Dr Harty Cup and the All-Ireland colleges title, so it was a big year for us.

After that, I moved on to under-21 hurling and football, and I captained Cork to win the under-21 hurling in 1976 – I had the honour as Sars had won

THE ACTION

★★★★★

KERRY SEEMED SET for victory as they held a two-point lead late on, but a high ball into Kingdom territory was won by an attacker, who turned and fired home a winning goal. Offaly's Séamus Darby in 1982? No, Cork's Tadhg Murphy in 1983.

Cork were without Tom Creedon. In May of 1983 he suffered grave injuries in a van accident, saving the life of his son, Tom Jnr. Tragically, the Macroom man would die in August of that year.

The home side showed they were up for it, with John Cleary and Dinny Allen on target early on, and then combining for a goal as Allen provided the assist for the teenager to slot the ball beyond Charlie Nelligan. It was 1-5 each at the interval.

Four minutes into the new half, Cork had another goal. Again, Allen was involved – this time his sideline kick was not dealt with by the Kerry defence and Murphy foreshadowed his later intervention by scrambling the loose ball home. Kerry managed to move ahead for the first time with a goal from a penalty by Jack O'Shea and a Mikey Sheehy point. When Kerry sub Seán Walsh landed a goal on the hour, with Sheehy once again tacking on a point, Micky O'Dwyer's men led by four.

Cleary pointed in the 65th minute to leave a goal in it. Murphy added another. When Cork won a free out the field in injury time, Tadhg O'Reilly launched the ball towards the goalmouth, and Murphy did the rest.

★★★★★

the under-21 county in 1975. That same year, I was briefly part of the senior football panel. Then I was called on to the hurling team for 1977, and I came on for Gerald McCarthy when he got injured in the All-Ireland final that year when we beat Wexford. His injury was kind of fortunate for me as it guaranteed I'd get a medal, but I was only there for the year, though – I got injured in the '77 All-Ireland under-21 final and that knocked me back a bit. I went back to playing both codes club-wise, Sarsfields in hurling and Glanmire in football, before I was called up for the football again in 1981.

Hurling was always my preference, to be honest about it, but I enjoyed playing football immensely and it was strong in East Cork at the time – I won county senior football championship medals with the divisional team, Imokilly, in 1984 and '86.

As well as the under-21 hurling win in 1976, we had reached the All-Ireland final in '75 and '77, but in the under-21 football I had played against Kerry for three years and lost to them in each of those. It was a similar situation at senior level – Cork had beaten Kerry in the 1974 Munster final, but Kerry went on to win eight in-a-row after that and it was a fairly frustrating time.

In 1982, for example, we drew with them in the National League final in Killarney and they beat us in the replay in Páirc Uí Chaoimh; then, we drew with them in the Munster final down the Páirc and they beat us in the replay in Killarney. That gave us an indication that we were quite close to Kerry at the time, and we felt that we were capable of beating them on a given day but, when we were beaten, we were gone for the year.

That was tough, whereas in today's world you'd have a couple of chances.

Obviously, Kerry had lost to Offaly in the 1982 All-Ireland final when they were going for five in-a-row. Whenever we had played them, we went out hoping to give a performance – whether it was good enough or not – but that result definitely gave us a pointer that we had a chance. It was a case of everybody working hard and hoping that we got the break, something which didn't always happen against them.

Eamonn Ryan, who would go on to have so much success with the Cork ladies' football team, was the manager of the team. He had been there in 1982, and for '83 they brought in Joe McGrath – after whom the McGrath Cup, the secondary football competition in Munster, was named. I don't know what he was described as back then, but he was essentially the coach. He was a great character; he was a motivating and psychological kind of operator. He'd kind of instil in you that you were maybe a bit better than you thought you were!

I remember the first time we met Joe… it was a league game up in the North, against Down or Derry. We had a meeting on the Saturday night and Joe was introduced to the team. He gave one of his usual rousing speeches and one of his lines was, 'If you listen to McGrath and do what he tells you, in three months you'll be fifty percent a better player than starting out'. John Allen was next to me and he gave me a poke in the shoulder.

'Jesus!' he said, 'There won't be a team in the country to keep the ball kicked out to us this year!' In fairness, everybody enjoyed Joe and he dovetailed well with Eamonn.

After 1982, we felt that we weren't too far away, but in '83 we struggled in the Munster semi-final against Clare up in Cusack Park. That was a very close game and it was only towards the end that we got away from them – I got a late goal and a couple of points, and Dinny Allen might have got a few scores. It dragged us over the line in a way but it brought us into the Munster final as major underdogs. In a way, that was probably a good thing because, deep down, we knew that we were capable of a performance. We were well up for the final, to be honest about it. A lot of people mightn't have expected that but we were still looking back at 1982 and drawing with them twice. We were waiting in the high grass to have another go at them.

The grass grew even higher the day of the Munster final – it was the middle of July, but it poured with rain the same day. I went to Mass in the local church in Glanmire – Springhill, we call it – and we couldn't come out afterwards, the rain was so bad. Mick Dunne from RTÉ was actually at Mass there too and we ended up chatting for a second and he said, 'There's no way this game is going to go ahead'.

It was torrential at the time, a very bad thunder-and-lightning morning. There was a bit of a doubt, but the sun came out eventually. Even getting to the game, going down Centre Park Road there was flooding and it was hard to get down. We were meeting at Blackrock's ground and we had to take a roundabout method to get there.

I had been named at wing-forward and I started the game with Mick Spillane marking me, though Denis 'Ogie' Moran was moved back to mark me during the match. I had marked Páidí Ó Sé in the league and, no matter who it was, you knew you were in for a tough day. We had a strong forward line – Eoin O'Mahony from Clonakilty was centre-forward and Dave Barry was on the other wing. John Allen was full-forward, he was a good target-man… and then John Cleary in one corner and Dinny in the other, so there was good scoring potential there, whichever way you looked at it.

We were all up for it, definitely, and one of the things that gave us a big boost was that there had been a big doubt about our full-back, Kevin Kehilly but he was assessed that morning and came through. He was a big leader in that group, so that he was available gave us a massive lift. Kevin played very well on the day; the man who missed out was John Fouhy from Kildorrery, who was a very good player, and it was tough on him.

It was nip-and-tuck for most of the game, we stayed with them for a lot of it. At one stage, it seemed as if Kerry were getting into a bit of a stride in the second-half and would drift away, but no, we were hanging in there and they just couldn't get four or five points ahead of us. I scored a goal in the second-half – and it was key that we were always within striking distance. It was 3-9 to 2-10 for them as time was running out.

My recall of the goal is as clear as ever.

Dinny was fouled and he got up as if he was going to take the free, but it was lucky he didn't… and Tadhg O'Reilly just let rip. One thing the Kerry lads didn't appreciate was how long the ball was going to land in from Tadhg, because he had a huge kick of a dead ball. I just had that extra step to get off the ground and the fact that I knew how far it was going to come and where it was going to land was the secret.

When I saw Tadhg taking the free, I knew it was going to clear the lot of them… and that's what happened. I just made the right call at the right time.

I caught the ball to the right of the City End goal as I was looking at it. I kept the shot low and it hit the far post… and rolled back across and in. Dinny said afterwards that it felt like an eternity watching the ball hit the upright – would it come back out or go in?

The relief when it went in was unbelievable! You couldn't have scripted it better. Once Charlie took the kickout, John Moloney called for the ball… and that was it. You always feared that, if they had the chance to get back, they would.

We met Dublin in the All-Ireland semi-final and, after drawing with them in Croke Park, Cork County Board managed to get the replay in Páirc Uí Chaoimh, but they beat us. That was disappointing, especially as we felt that we had the measure of them the first day, but it just didn't happen. We'd have loved to go all the way but it wasn't to be.

Because of the rain, there was only a small crowd there, 16,000 or 17,000, maybe… but with the amount of people who've come up to me to tell me they were there, it feels like 60,000 or 70,000! One morning a few years ago, I was in Canty's pub in Cork city having a coffee and a man came up to me and asked if I was Tadhg Murphy?

I said I was, and he said he was glad to have met me. He had been out on an oil rig with three Kerry guys and it was one of the happiest moments of his life! There are pockets of real hardcore Cork football support who had to put up with a lot of heartache against Kerry, and for them it was great. I think everybody enjoyed it on the day, especially the way it happened. Of course, nobody was happier than Mrs Moynihan in the Long Valley!

The goal got a lot of attention again when Cork beat Kerry in 2020, especially as Mark Keane's winning goal was right at the death and at the same end as mine. Claire Byrne of RTÉ had me on the radio and the whole thing erupted again; it was a bit of craic anyway.

It's not something I'll ever get tired of talking about – it was one of those moments that you have to cherish and I was lucky to have experienced it. But even beyond that one match and the goal, it was a great team to be involved with. Mick Burns, who tragically died in 2015, was one of my best friends on the team and what a character he was – every night at training, he'd have some story for us.

Because Mick was from Castlehaven down in West Cork, we might go a long while without seeing each other, but not long before he died, he called into Sars' clubhouse one evening, as he was working up around that part of the world at the time. We had a good chat and it's something I was very grateful for when I found out he had died.

Obviously, when your time with the county is over, you go back playing with the club, but it's nice to keep the connection with the lads that you played with for Cork.

You never lose that bond.

★ ★ ★ ★ ★

JOHN CLEARY

66

WE HAD WON the All-Ireland minor in 1981; then in '82 we won the Munster under-21 and maybe should have gone on to win that All-Ireland, but we were beaten by Roscommon in the All-Ireland semi-final – they got two late goals. It was a game played in very bad conditions, and we did well that day but they caught us. The second goal was in the last minute and we had no chance to come back.

The league started in October of 1982, and I broke in then. I was still only 19 and myself and Eoin O'Mahony were drafted in. It was probably a bit of a surprise but, to be honest, you just go with the flow, really. When we had been successful at minor and under-21, it's just a natural progression and you don't think about age or anything like that.

Cork had actually drawn twice with Kerry in 1982. The league final in Killarney was a draw and Kerry won by four in the replay in Páirc Uí Chaoimh. The Munster final in the Páirc finished 0-9 each, but Kerry then won by 2-18 to 0-12 back at home, everyone expecting them to go on and do the five in-a-row.

The 1982-83 league went fairly well – we finished third in Division 1, but it was only two teams who went forward to the knockout stages. The league had gone well for me and I'd got a good few scores. We had beaten Offaly, the All-Ireland champions, and had some good games under our belts. We felt that we had a good enough team, but obviously you were going up against a superstar Kerry side.

Then, we beat Clare in the Munster semi-final by 1-11 to 1-5, but it was a lot closer than that. We got a few late scores and we could very easily have been beaten that day. At that time, Clare, Limerick, Tipperary or Waterford wouldn't usually get close to Cork or Kerry, so we were going into the final almost being written off, especially as Kerry were going for nine in-a-row in Munster. There was no Munster senior medal in our team.

Joe McGrath would be a great man to build confidence.

He'd do anything if he thought it would improve the set-up, and Eamonn Ryan then was a great coach. There was no lack of belief going in and because it was knockout football with no back door, you'd always give Cork a chance, even going back to the late 70s when Kerry seemed unbeatable.

We weren't without hope, but all the pundits were expecting Kerry to win comfortably. They were after being beaten by Offaly in the previous year's All-Ireland… the famous Séamus Darby goal, and they were itching to get back.

The heavens opened on the morning of the match, an awful thunderstorm. The team was meeting in Blackrock and I was travelling up from Castlehaven with the late Mick Burns, who was a sub. I can remember we had to try two or three ways to get there, as the roads were flooded. Then, having finally made it there, there was talk that the game mightn't be played at all! It eased considerably by match-time, thankfully.

At that time, a Munster final was nearly always a sell-out but there was a crowd of only around 17,000 or so there that day. The weather in the morning was a factor and maybe the fact that Cork weren't being given a lot of hope, people didn't travel as they expected it to be one-way traffic.

The fact that we weren't being given a chance was probably a help inside in the camp. We were going in as no-hopers, but there had been a few other young fellas brought into the panel. Colman Corrigan was just starting at that time as well along with myself and Eoin, and we were used to beating Kerry. We were under no pressure whatsoever – it was a case of going out, doing your level best and seeing where it took you.

I was named at corner-forward, being marked by Ger O'Keeffe. John Allen was full-forward and Dinny Allen was in the other corner. Being young, you don't give too much notice to who's going to be on you – you're just looking forward to it as a great occasion. When you're 19, you're expecting that you'll be there for a good few years, so there was no huge expectation or pressure.

That day, I was lucky enough in that Dinny Allen broke a great ball after 10 or 12 minutes and I got a goal – the one that nobody remembers! I ran into space and took a chance, and it broke in front of me. I saw Charlie Nelligan coming out, I slipped it along the ground and luckily it went in.

It was great to get a confidence boost like that early on, and we were level at half-time, 1-6 each. Even though Kerry had come back with a goal and a point before the break, the crowd in the old covered stand were absolutely roaring us on, because we were well in it when some people might have thought the game would be over by half-time.

We got a huge boost out of that going in at the break. Joe McGrath was always full of positivity and I remember him saying, 'Look lads, everyone said ye had no chance but here ye are'. In the second-half, we just kept at it.

Tadhgie got his first goal early on, and we stayed in touch. We actually played very well but it looked like Kerry were going to get over the line. That said, they missed a couple of scores at the end to put it from two... to three to four. We had played so well to be close that the bit of luck came then at the end.

Dinny Allen was fouled and he put the ball down, as all frees had to be taken from the ground at that time. I was standing behind him and I was looking in, just about to take it. Next thing... Tadhg O'Reilly came from behind the two of us to whip it in. The rest then was Tadhgie Murphy. It was unbelievable, really.

It was grand for me, as it was my first year, but this was great for the older lads, who had been beaten by Kerry over the previous eight years. There were huge celebrations.

We had Dublin in the All-Ireland semi-final in Croke Park and we played out of our skins; it was a game we should have won, but they got a draw out of it. It was an opportunity missed – the luck that we had against Kerry, we didn't have against Dublin... so it's swings and roundabouts.

The replay was in Páirc Uí Chaoimh and it was the first time all year that there was a bit of pressure on us. Things didn't go our way that day and it was a regret. I think if we had beaten Dublin, we'd have had a great chance against Galway in the final as the team was getting better and better.

The important thing was that we had ended the run against Kerry, though.

99

CONOR COUNIHAN
(& COLMAN CORRIGAN)

CORK 0-13 ★ **KERRY 1-5**
Munster SFC Final Replay
Fitzgerald Stadium, Killarney
AUGUST 2, 1987

★ **CORK:** J Kerins; T Davis (0-2), **C Corrigan**, D Walsh; N Cahalane, **C Counihan**, T Nation (0-1); S Fahy (0-1), T McCarthy (0-1); P Hayes, L Tompkins (0-4), J Kerrigan; J O'Driscoll (0-1), C Ryan, J Cleary (0-2). **Subs:** T Leahy (0-1) for Hayes, D Culloty for Kerrigan.

★ **KERRY:** C Nelligan; P Ó Sé, S Walsh, M Spillane; T Doyle (0-1), T Spillane, G Lynch; D Hanifin (1-0), A O'Donovan; J Kennedy, J O'Shea (0-2), P Spillane; M Sheehy (0-1), E Liston, G Power. **Subs:** T O'Dowd for Kennedy, M McAuliffe for O'Dowd, V O'Connor (0-1) for O'Donovan.

66

THERE WAS A real sense that Cork, with all of the minor and under-21 success, were coming on strong and that Kerry were on the wane – some people would say that we should have toppled them before we actually did!

Having that belief that we could beat Kerry was probably the last part of the jigsaw, and Billy Morgan was ideal for us in that regard. He had the passion and the drive for it and he was able to inspire others.

Like most clubs in East Cork, Aghada would have had a good focus on hurling, but I came up with a good underage team, successful all the way up in football. We were beaten in a county under-14 final after a replay – I was captain, and it was one of the lowest points of my whole career! We won the under-16 and that same team got to the final of the county section of the minor – back then, the

THE ACTION

★★★★★

IN BILLY MORGAN'S first year in charge of the Cork senior football team, they seemed set to make a breakthrough as they led Kerry with time running out in the Munster final at Páirc Uí Chaoimh.

However, champions die hard and Kerry, after the disappointments of 1982 and '83, had roared back to win three more All-Irelands. Despite being second-best for most of the provincial decider on the banks of the Lee, they looked to have saved things at the death with Mikey Sheehy's late goal at the City End.

Standing at the endline, Morgan fell to his knees in dismay. However, the man who was now wearing the Cork No 1 jersey that was once the property of Morgan displayed swift thinking. John Kerins took a quick kick-out, Cork were handed a chance to draw after a foul on John O'Driscoll, and Larry Tompkins kept his nerve to nail the free and send the tie to a replay in Killarney.

Quite simply, there was only one side in the second game – it took Kerry 33 minutes to get on the scoreboard, a Mikey Sheehy free, by which time Cork were six points to the good. The home side had shot 11 wides by half-time.

With captain Conor Counihan dominant at centre-back, Cork were well on top, aided by Ger Power's first-half sending-off for a late tackle on Tony Davis – insult was added to injury when Davis scored two points as the spare man.

★★★★★

winners of the county and the winners of the city would play in the county final proper. We had beaten Knocknagree and a Beara team that had three county minors, but we lost to Macroom, and then St Finbarr's beat them.

We went on at under-21 and won a couple of East Cork titles. A lot of the team moved up to adult level then and if you have one group that wins a bit, it drives everything on. We won a junior league in 1979 and the divisional championship in '80 – we actually won an East Cork hurling and football double that year. We were beaten by Ballincollig in the county final. In 1981, we won another East Cork and were beaten in the semi-final by a point against Kilmurry. In 1983, we were beaten by St Nick's second team after two draws.

It took until 1989 to win the county junior – we beat Knocknagree after a replay in the final – and then in '91 we won the intermediate, getting revenge over Ballincollig 10 ten years previous. Our first year up senior, we made it to the county semi-final and we were beaten by O'Donovan Rossa. They went on to not only win the county, but also Munster and the All-Ireland!

As an underage player, I was okay without standing out. There was a man in the club, Willie Ryan, who was a selector for the Imokilly minor team and he asked me to come to trials. I would have played corner-back at the time, but they had no goalkeeper and I was asked to stand in for a game against Avondhu. I got two or three balls in and laid them out, no fuss.

After that, a combined Avondhu/Imokilly team was being picked to play Waterford and I was one of only two Imokilly fellas chosen. Unfortunately, I lasted about 25 minutes – five goals had gone past me by then!

That was the end of my goalkeeping career!

In the late 1970s, I was diagnosed as a coeliac. That used to impact me in terms of a lack of energy but after the diagnosis I began to improve. In my second-last year at under-21, 1979, I was on the extended Cork squad that reached the All-Ireland final, losing to Down, but I never made a match-day panel. In 1980, I had to battle to get into the team, but I was picked at corner-back and I played every game in the championship. We beat Dublin in the All-Ireland final, and it was a good Dublin team as five of them won All-Irelands in 1983 – Barney Rock, Ciarán Duff, Jim Ronayne, John O'Leary and PJ Buckley.

When the 1980-81 National League started in the autumn, I was called on to the senior panel. I played a few games and made my championship debut in a win over Waterford in 1981 but I didn't come off the bench for the Munster final down in Killarney – Kerry won by 1-11 to 0-3. I was dropped off the panel after that and it looked like that was it for my inter-county career.

Football was very strong in East Cork at the time and that meant that Imokilly, the divisional team, did well. Aghada were still junior and you had Glanmire, who had experienced guys like Tadhg and Bertie Óg Murphy and Teddy McCarthy. Then there was Midleton – Kevin Hennessy and Denis Mulcahy played hurling for Cork but they were very good footballers, and Ger Glavin was on the fringes of the football panel.

They had all played at high levels and could deal with big occasions. There were other guys then, like Kieran Murphy from Castlemartyr – he was small, but he was powerful. Fellas were determined to make the most of the chances we had and we were big physically, too.

We made it to the county final in 1984 and beat St Finbarr's. I was captain of that team and the county champions used to be allowed to nominate a selector for the following year, so it was inevitable we'd have one or two players chosen. That winter, I felt I'd get a shot so I made sure to do an awful lot of work. When I got the kick in the ass of being dropped, it drove me on and made me all the keener to take the second chance. A while back, I was talking to a scout from Crystal Palace, who told me they often take chances on guys who haven't made it elsewhere but keep plugging away – they have resilience, that chip on the shoulder, and I was the same.

By this stage, I was playing at centre-back. A corner-back learns his game back there, how to read the play, and centre-back was very much about reading, so it was a logical move. I'd have been well aware that I wasn't the fastest fella around, so hopefully the ability to read it helped me in that regard. You might watch a bit of the guy you were going to be marking, but video analysis didn't really exist. In the old-school way, it was all about watching your man and doing your job. Looking at football today, I get worried that nobody is watching anyone! While collective defending can be good, the ability of fellas to defend one-on-one now is questionable and there's still plenty of room for it, in my view. We didn't have the comfort of a blanket defence back then!

As Imokilly had the right to choose the captain too, I was given that role for 1985 – Kerry beat us in the Munster final in Páirc Uí Chaoimh – and I kept my place on the team after that. Imokilly won the county again in 1986, and I was nominated as captain again for '87. Being captain didn't bring too much in the way of extra responsibility – I always kind of looked at myself as someone who was lucky to be there, in a sense. Once you did your best on the field and led by example in training, I felt that that was enough. In terms of big speeches or anything like that, that wouldn't be my forte at all.

The feeling after the draw with Kerry in Páirc Uí Chaoimh was strange. We had to get the late equaliser but, rather than feeling that we had been lucky to get a second chance, we were full sure that we'd finish the job in the replay. Kerry were on the cliff-edge and we just had to stamp on their hands.

I can't remember a lot of the finer details of the replay but it did feel fairly comfortable for much of it. Winning it in Killarney was extra special. With the best will in the world, we needed a bit of luck to win in 1983, whereas this couldn't be disputed. It felt like the beginning of something.

That said, we played Galway in the semi-final afterwards and we were fairly lucky to come out of that with a draw. There was a minute to go and we were a point down – Dandy Kelly came through the middle for Galway and there was a fella to my right, a pass that would surely have led to another point… but he passed it straight to me. I kicked it out the wing, to where Larry was fouled. It was a tough kick, more than 50 metres out, but he landed it over and we were well over them in the replay.

Meath beat us in the All-Ireland final. On a personal level, when you're captain of a team that gets that far and loses, it's a fairly low ebb. Then, the competitive nature in you comes out again and you say, *F**k this, I'm going back there again and we're going to sort this.* When we came back to Cork on the Monday night, we went to the offices of *The Cork Examiner* and *Evening Echo* and I stood on the balcony outside, facing out to the huge crowd on St Patrick's St and told them we'd be back the following year with Sam Maguire. I was out by a year!

You tend to say those things. I can remember in 2009, when I was manager after we lost to Kerry in the All-Ireland final – on the Monday morning, we were fairly hungover and, before we left the hotel, I pulled them all into a room. 'We're going down here tonight,' I said, 'and we're going to hold our heads up f**king high and we're going to be back here next year'.

Did I really believe that at the time? I don't know, but if you're to lead, you have to show that leadership. If you don't give off that impression, what hope have you?

Is it better to win an All-Ireland as a player than as a manager? I suppose everything is relative at your stage of life. For us, having lost 1987 and '88, beating Mayo in '89 was a relief, because our ability to win it had been questioned. Then, you go on the following year and it's Meath – if you don't win that, the previous year isn't worth anything!

Nothing substitutes for playing, but there is an awful lot of satisfaction in managing a group to win one – and to be fortunate enough to have such a group that were very easy to manage. Don't get me wrong, I had moments with players, but they were very much self-driven.

The amount of time and effort they put in was phenomenal. If I had those fellas working in an organisation, I could shut the door and know that the show would go on.

★ ★ ★ ★ ★

COLMAN CORRIGAN

"

I WAS ONLY 16 when I first played at adult level, in 1979. It wouldn't be allowed nowadays and my parents had to be asked for permission for me to be allowed to play. My father said, 'Look, if ye think he's good enough, ye play him'.

We won the intermediate – which was then the second tier – and the county under-21 in 1982, so we had a very good panel of players and we played at senior level until 1987. By that stage, the older lads from 1982 had gone and some of the under-21 team had emigrated and things like that.

Macroom always had a strong tradition and in 1983 there were four of us in the Cork squad. There was the great Tom Creedon, who was to tragically die that year, Mick Moloney, Barry Lynch and myself.

When I was in the Cork minor set-up, we went down to play Glanmire in Blarney – and we forgot our jerseys! We had to wear the Blarney jerseys, which were red and white, the same as Cork. As I was going to my position at wing-back, one of my best friends, the goalkeeper, Tim O'Sullivan, passed me and quipped, 'Don't forget who you're playing for – it might be red and white, but you're still playing for Macroom!' That was bred in to us at that time; that your club was first… always and ever.

We had a cracking Cork minor team in 1979, absolutely brilliant; players like Dave Barry, Ephie Fitzgerald, the late Mick Burns from Castlehaven… Martin Connolly. We were brutally unfortunate – Ambrose O'Donovan scored a last-minute goal for Kerry to draw in the Munster final in Killarney and they beat the shit out of us in the replay and went on to win the All-Ireland. The following year, we were beaten by Kerry in the Munster final again, having been up by 0-9 to 0-2 after quarter of an hour.

I went straight in to under-21 in 1981 and we won the All-Ireland. The following year, we lost to Roscommon – another last-minute goal – and I was captain in 1983 when we lost to Kerry by a point. The year before I came on the under-21 panel, 1980, Cork had won the All-Ireland at that grade and three more followed from 1984-86, so the county won five titles in seven years. That was huge in terms of what followed.

I'm lucky enough to have a spot below in Derrynane, Co. Kerry and the locals will often throw out the view that, only for Larry Tompkins and Shea Fahy, Cork would have won nothing. My counter-argument to that, and I'll always believe it, is that Larry and Shea wouldn't have anything only for us!

Don't get me wrong, Larry and Shea were phenomenal and they contributed massively, but we still had won five under-21s in seven years. You had the likes of Teddy Mac, Mick Mac, Tony Davis, Danny Culloty, Mick Slocum, Niall Cahalane, John Cleary, Barry Coffey – what players they were! Then you added them to the so-called 'older' fellas like myself, the late Christy Ryan and Jimmy Kerrigan… it was binding all of those players together was the trick and that's where Billy Morgan came in. At the same time, there was a reasonable expectation on us to perform.

In 1983, we had been unlucky after beating Kerry. We should have beaten

Dublin in the All-Ireland semi-final and then in the replay it was the Brian Mullins' show. I was midfield that day and the physicality was frightening.

Denis Coughlan had trained us in 1985 and '86, and then he pulled out. Billy came home and he was appointed coach-manager, but not a selector, as hard as that might be to believe now. We were absolutely thrilled that Billy was there and, anything that he said, we took on board 100 percent. He always said that, once we crossed the white line it was up to us, but his coaching and his managerial skills were superb. He got Frank Cogan in, ostensibly as masseur, but he did a lot of the coaching too.

During the 1986-87 league, we started gaining confidence. Of course, the 1987 quarter-final against Dublin was the infamous day where we walked off when the match was a draw at full-time, and Barney Rock scored a goal into an empty net in extra time. There has been a lot written and said about it but the simple reason we didn't come back out was because Billy thought there was a replay, and he wanted to get an extra game into us as a young team coming up. We had plenty of fun out of that episode, but we also used it as a motivating factor.

Then you have Shea and Larry coming on the scene, and you ally them with the guys coming up. Something that people mightn't realise though is that, where we gained Shea and Larry for 1987, we were still without Dave Barry and Dinny Allen. They missed 1985, '86 and '87.

We were drawn against Limerick in the 1987 Munster semi-final and it was a game where everyone was expecting them to roll us over, but we were really lucky to come out of it. We won by six points but it meant that Kerry were raging-hot favourites for the Munster final. They had won the last three All-Irelands and I know for a fact, from speaking to Kerry lads I'm friendly with, they were gung-ho about winning another four in-a-row. They reckoned that, if they got over Cork, there wasn't a whole lot else to stop them. Meath were coming but Kerry had beaten them well in 1986.

We played really well that day in the Páirc but, of course, Mikey Sheehy got the last-minute goal to put them a point up. John Kerins, God be good to him, the quick-thinking guy that he was, took a fast kickout − practically from his hands, the ball hardly touched the ground... more like a drop-kick than anything! John O'Driscoll got it and won a free, which Larry put over.

Even still, everybody in the stand said that that was Cork's chance gone. You never get the chance to beat Kerry twice was the attitude: if you don't beat them the first day, you're f**ked.

When the goal went in, Billy was standing behind the endline and fell to his knees. By the time he got into the dressing-room, we had gotten hold of the situation inside. When he came in and saw us, he said, 'We're going to win the replay!' Billy had given us huge belief and confidence since he had come in and that moment was a manifestation of that; the players had no doubt that we were going down to Killarney and winning.

The replay was just a week later, on the August bank holiday Sunday, but it wasn't an issue – Billy had us absolutely incredibly fit; there was no other team in as good a shape as us. It wasn't a big deal; we had a good kickaround on the Tuesday.

We went to the Castlerosse Hotel beforehand and from there up to the stadium. There was a good crowd around – Cork fans would always be good to travel to Killarney, in fairness – and I can never remember a game where I was so sure we were going to win. There was just that feeling that fellas were going to step up.

Back then, you were nearly five points down before the ball was thrown in against Kerry, but for the replay it wasn't like that; it was totally different. In the first quarter of an hour, there was good belting going in and individual battles being won and that's what we had to do: you couldn't leave a Mikey Sheehy or a Bomber Liston dominate, because they'd punish you.

I had played wing-back and centre-back for the Cork minor team and the under-21s. Then, the last year at under-21, 1983 – I was put in full-back. Whether somebody was looking at Kevin Kehilly in the senior team and doing some succession-planning, I don't know. I played midfield for the seniors in 1983 and '84, then Kevin retired and I was moved to full-back for '85.

I didn't mind the lack of freedom. I loved the sense of going in to battle against full-forwards and you had a lot of them who were decent around that time. Backs play is completely different now – there's no full-backs! It feels like it's easier to play there now, because you've so many people in front of you.

Billy used to allow lads have a couple of pints the night before a match, but I liked to go for a walk and clear the head, get up early then and set my sights from around 9am. You'd visualise the ball coming in – *Which side am I going to show him? Which foot am I fastest off?* When Jack O'Shea got the ball, the first fella he would always look for was the Bomber. If he came out, you'd have Sheehy or John Egan peeling around on the loop.

My first time marking the Bomber was the 1985 Munster final in Páirc Uí Chaoimh. You'd be fairly good and nervous, because this could finish your career – he had finished plenty of them. The first ball comes in and he wins it out in front of me; I slip on my ass and he kicks it over the bar. You're thinking, *Here we go*, but I recovered. You have to focus on the individual duel and that's what we did in 1987.

The Bomber's first 20 metres were blistering – he wouldn't be able to sustain it, but you had to stay with him. I was lucky enough to be fast off the mark anyway, so that was a plus. The main thing was not to let him inside you, because if you did, you were in trouble.

The game was almost won in the first 20 minutes… we were up 0-7 to 0-2. I say 'almost' because Kerry were still *Kerry*, but I remember Billy saying to us that, if the tide looked like it was turning, to start a fight. Tony Davis and Ger Power had a set-to by the sideline in front of the stand and Billy got involved in it – basically saying, *Remember what I said to ye!* Once we weathered Kerry's storm for three or four minutes, we were back at it again. They couldn't break us down.

Power was sent off later and Tony was the spare man as we saw out the game. With all due respect, the last 10 minutes were just a feeling of having finally done it. Teddy McCarthy and Shea Fahy were brilliant at midfield, so dominant that Kerry moved Jacko to centre-forward. We were nearly able to showboat – nobody did, but that's how it felt.

The scenes at the end were phenomenal and completely different to 1983. When we won in '83, there was a very small crowd there and only half of them were from Cork. In 1987, you had a hell of a lot more, even if not all of them had travelled in the expectation of a Cork win!

There was a bus outside the dressing-room and we were meant to get on that after the match and head back to Castlerosse. Morgan came into the room and said, 'F**k the bus, we're walking through the town!'

There was a bar here in Macroom called Browne's. It's closed down now but a lot of people met their future spouses there! I was best friends with Kerinsie and we agreed to meet there on the way back from Killarney. Some of us ended up in the International Hotel and the place was absolutely lifting.

Kerinsie went into one car and I went into another, with friends of mine. He went to Browne's…and I ended up at Páidí Ó Sé's pub in Ventry as my buddies were staying there for the bank holiday weekend. Kerinsie didn't talk to me for a week after it!

In hindsight, I suppose it was difficult for us to reset and re-focus for the All-Ireland semi-final against Galway – and we damn nearly threw it away. As the replay showed, we were 10 points a better team than Galway, even though they had some fine players, but our attitude going in was totally wrong. We would have been caught only for Larry's late equaliser.

In the final then, Meath had a bit more experience and we were maybe a bit naïve going into it, even though we had a fantastic start. Going on from that, I believe that we needed to win a national title before we could become All-Ireland champions. In that regard, winning the league in 1989 was vital for us. The feeling was, *We can do it… now, let's go on and do the next big one.*

After we beat Dublin in the 'home' league final, we went to New York to play them over two legs in the league final proper. Unfortunately, I ruptured my Achilles tendon while we were over there, from my ankle to right up behind my knee, and lost an inch and a half of my calf muscle.

The doctor in New York told me to forget about ever again playing sport. When Dr Con Murphy heard that, he refused to accept it and said to come away home. When we landed in Shannon, there was an escort waiting for me and I was whisked down to Tralee while the boys continued their celebrations.

It was an operation that hadn't been done before in Ireland. Fionán O'Carroll was doing it and he told me it was the biggest one he had done, and he didn't know how it was going to work out. It was tough to hear but at the same time I appreciated the honesty. He set out a plan and I got to it afterwards and, to be fair, I haven't ever had pain in it since.

Due to my rehabilitation, I obviously didn't play any part in the championship, as Cork finally won Sam. People always ask me if that made it bittersweet and, of course, it did, but shit happens. I was delighted to have been part of that set-up. In that group, nobody was ever left out – if you were number 26 or number 1, we were all treated the same.

I had been working in insurance at the time with the Construction Industry Federation but I couldn't drive for six months and lost the job. I had got married in 1987 and had a mortgage of 16 percent – a week after the operation, I was sitting at home on a Wednesday morning, feeling sorry for myself, when there was a shadow at the door, ringing the bell. I opened it… and it was Billy.

The first thing he asked was, why I hadn't been at training the previous night? I tried to explain that I had a plaster-cast all the way up my leg, but he just said, 'Don't you ever again miss a training session', turned on his heel and sat into his car and left. I was at every single training session after that. I even gave the talk in the dressing-room before the final. One thing I remember saying was that Mayo were maybe a bit like we had been in 1987, a bit naïve and a bit frightened.

In 1990, I actually played against Limerick, which proved to be my last championship match with Cork, but I never stopped pushing for a place, which hopefully brought the best out in the fellas who had the jerseys. Coming up to the All-Ireland final, I was playing very well in the practice games. We played Kerry in one of those, down in Killarney; they put Pat Spillane in on me, and I beat him up a stick.

The whole panel pushed each other and we were all friends. It's kind of scary to think that five of that panel are gone now – Kerinsie, Mick Mac, Teddy Mac, Mick Burns and Christy Ryan. The bond stays strong, though. At Teddy's funeral in 2023, we were all there and went down to The Castle Bar in Glanmire afterwards. Obviously, you'll have different groups within the group but we all get on and there's plenty of ball-hopping and slagging, and our wives get on.

They were great times and it's only looking back that people properly appreciate how good it was.

PAUL McGRATH

CORK 1–12 ★ **KERRY 1–9**
Munster SFC Final
Fitzgerald Stadium
JULY 23, 1989

★ **CORK:** J Kerins; S O'Brien, D Walsh, K Kerrigan; T Davis, C Counihan, B Coffey; S Fahy, L Tompkins (0-7); T McCarthy, D Barry, J O'Driscoll (1-1); **P McGrath (0-2)**, D Allen (0-1), J Cleary (0-1). **Sub:** M Slocum for Walsh.

★ **KERRY:** C Nelligan; K Savage, A O'Donovan (1-0), M Spillane; C Murphy, T Doyle, M Nix; J O'Shea, T Spillane; T Fleming, M Fitzgerald (0-6), J Shannon; W Maher, E Liston (0-1), P Spillane (0-2). **Subs:** A Gleeson for M Spillane, M McAuliffe for Shannon, P Dennehy for Maher.

66

IT WAS EARLY 1985. I was in my first year in UCC and I was on the Sigerson Cup panel. Mick O'Dwyer was training us and he came up to me one day after training.

'Paul, your mother's from Kenmare?'

'Yeah, she is… yeah.'

'And were you born in Tralee?'

'I was.'

'Would you be interested in playing with us?'

Now, Micko wasn't a fella who'd be above having a laugh, so I was looking at him, unsure of how to react. I asked him who 'us' was, just to be clear, and he confirmed that he meant Kerry and he was serious. 'Would you come training with us anyway?' he asked.

THE ACTION

★★★★★

NEVER BEFORE HAD Cork managed to win three consecutive Munster SFC titles, but it underlined the increase in expectations that this in itself was not a cause for major celebration. Victory in Killarney was a means to an end – after losses to Meath in the All-Ireland finals of 1987 and '88 (after a replay), only winning Sam Maguire was enough now.

Before a crowd of 47,011, Kerry enjoyed a good start as they moved into a 0-4 to 0-1 lead, while Cork lost full-back Denis Walsh to injury, but substitute Mick Slocum made a good impact. The Rebels battled back to tie at 0-4 each but they would have conceded a goal but for a great Larry Tompkins intervention to stop Maurice Fitzgerald getting on the end of a Timmy Fleming pass.

Cork moved in front with a Dinny Allen point and O'Driscoll's goal, well set up by Barry Coffey, was followed by a Paul McGrath point as Cork retired with a 1-7 to 0-6 half-time advantage.

A free and then a '45' from Tompkins on the resumption had Cork six clear, though they did heave a sigh of relief when Kerry's Eoin Liston failed to take advantage of a goal chance.

Kerry kept plugging away and were rewarded with a goal by Ambrose O'Donovan in the 70th minute. Somehow, there was just a score between the teams, but Cork repelled any attempts at a levelling goal for the home side.

★★★★★

I told him I didn't have a car – I was 19 and in first year of college – but he said that Ger Lynch from Valentia, who was wing-back on the Kerry team, was working up in the old mental hospital and he drove down on a Tuesday and a Thursday, and I could travel with him. I said I'd have to think about it – not in an arrogant way, but just to get my head around it. After all, I was someone who had never played at any level for Cork, and was being invited to train with Kerry, the then All-Ireland champions.

I went to Coláiste an Spioraid Naoimh in Bishopstown. Mick Kilcoyne, who played hurling for Westmeath, was our PE teacher – after moving down here, he hurled for Blackrock. We had won a Munster under-16B and he told us we were good enough to play Corn Uí Mhuirí. We probably didn't believe it at first, but he really drove us on. Guys like him were doing that with school teams in the 1980s but I don't see that same drive there now, and Cork football has suffered.

You look at Kerry's success over the last 20 years and you look at the Corn Uí Mhuirí roll of honour – Coláiste na Sceilge from Caherciveen, Tralee CBS, St Brendan's from Killarney and Dingle's Pobalscoil Chorca Dhuibhne have dominated it. They've produced the players and Cork colleges are not doing that anymore.

After Micko's invitation, I went home and talked about it with my father, Con; he was a garda from Galway, who had played for them and then transferred to Cork after being stationed down here – and he left it up to myself. Cork had won under-21 All-Irelands in 1980, '81 and '84, whereas Kerry had lost to Offaly in the 1982 All-Ireland final and then against Cork in '83. They had come back now (1984) to win the All-Ireland but, as far as I was concerned, that team was on the decline. As it happened, they went on to win another three in-a-row!

Even so, the future looked very bright from a Cork point of view. There was very good talent coming through and I reckoned that I should try to get into that stream, and I thanked Micko for the offer but thought it unrealistic from a number of points of view. I played Sigerson and I got a trial for Cork under-21s. Bob Honohan from Bishopstown was a selector and that probably didn't do me any harm.

I managed to get on the team – I was the free-taker, again probably thanks to Bob! – and we beat Derry in the All-Ireland final and I was pleased with the win and my contribution scoring five points. The following year (1986) we won again, beating Offaly in the final, and it underlined that, what I thought was true, was *true*. There was serious talent in Cork – Teddy McCarthy (RIP), Barry Coffey, Colm O'Neill, Mick Slocum, John O'Driscoll, John Murphy, Denis Walsh, Mick Maguire, Kevin Scanlon, Paddy Hayes, Con O'Connell, Mick McCarthy (RIP), Paddy Harrington… all on that team. That was my best game for Cork, scoring 1-7 in the final.

In 1987, we were going for what would have been four in-a-row in the grade and three in-a-row for me, but Tipperary beat us in the Munster semi-final in Páirc Uí Chaoimh.

By that stage – the 1986-87 academic year – Billy Morgan had succeeded Micko in training the UCC team. He had just taken over Cork too and asked me into the senior set-up for the first time. I trained with them for a while but then I broke my jaw in an inter-firm match and so, coupled with the under-21s, 1987 was a washout for me. Especially as, post-jaw-breaking recovery, in December, Bishopstown got to our first ever county under-21 final and were beaten by O'Donovan Rossa in a game we should never have lost.

Still, Cork reached the All-Ireland senior final for the first time since 1973, and Billy brought me along even though I had never played a senior game for Cork before that. My jaw was still wired up at the time and it was very uncomfortable – I was eating through a straw. I felt I had nothing to contribute and I told Billy that I didn't want to go, but he said, 'I want you to be there because you need to get the experience of an All-Ireland final set-up…and you're going to be there next year'. Hearing that was a big confidence-boost, the same as it had been to think that Micko thought I was up to a level at a time when I wasn't sure if I was.

Meath won in 1987, but Billy turned out to be right – we got to the final again in '88. I played wing-forward, albeit not very well I felt, but it went to a replay: I played worse and we lost again! There was probably an element of burnout – UCC had won the Sigerson in '88 and I had trained really hard for that, with my finals coming up at the same time. I had really pushed myself to try to get on the Cork team straight after that. I had probably trained too hard, on the go all the time, with club football factored in too. By the time the replay came, I was just whacked, physically and emotionally, and it showed.

After that, I resolved to listen to my body more, and I felt a lot stronger. It wasn't that I ducked training or took it easy and, if Billy thought you were pulling a fast one, he wouldn't be long putting you in your place, but I trained smarter and he was very accommodating – I'd rate him very highly as a good man-manager. The upshot was that I felt a lot stronger and played a lot better in 1989.

It probably helped that I settled at right corner-forward, too. The only time that I ever played in the left corner was when we played Roscommon in the 1990 semi-final. Colm O'Neill was in the right corner that day, with Shea Fahy full-forward, but right corner-forward was usually my position. It suited me – as long as there was good ball coming in! It was a totally different kind of game to now; back then, if you came out beyond the '45', there'd be fellas shouting at you to get back in!

When you were being marked in training by Niall Cahalane or Steven O'Brien or Tony Nation or Colman Corrigan, you weren't going to be worried by any other corner-back. To be fair, Bob O'Malley of Meath was excellent but he was right corner-back and I was right corner-forward, so we didn't come into contact much. Meath's left half-back, Martin O'Connell, was superb too – I was up against him in 1988 when I was right half-forward and he was at the top of his game. He was flying it and he made me look so bad, it wasn't funny! After that, the Cork management decided to push me into the corner!

We won the national league in 1989 (as my dad had, also with Cork, in 1952) and then we beat Tipp well in the Munster semi-final. That meant we were going down to Killarney for the final. The lads had beaten them there in the replay in 1987 and I made my championship debut when we played them on a wet day in the Páirc in 1988; we just got over the line with Dinny Allen getting a great goal. By 1989, we were going to Killarney, expecting to win.

There was a huge Cork crowd and the atmosphere was electric. It finished 1-12 to 1-9, and we probably won by less than we should have. Kerry came back and Ambrose O'Donovan got a goal towards the end to put a bit of respectability on the scoreboard, but we were well better than them.

The crowd and the buzz... that day was fabulous, better than any day in Croke Park. Obviously, Croke Park has a bigger capacity but a lot of neutrals go to All-Ireland finals, people from all 32 counties, and you have the commercialism now and the corporate boxes. There'll be vocal supporters there, of course, but you don't hear the support as focused as that day down in Killarney.

Definitely, my best game playing for Cork was the All-Ireland under-21 final in 1986. At senior level, probably the most effective game I played was the 1990 All-Ireland final. Colm was sent off, Mick Mc went off injured and Larry did his cruciate – I ended up doing a lot of running off the ball and making myself available as an outlet for the backs and the midfielders. We were down to 14 men for 50 minutes or so and it was all shoulders to the wheel.

The previous year, we had a full complement and it was easier to score; in 1990, it was a case of running 50 yards out the field to show for the ball and, at that stage then, you've a bit of work to do to get in towards the goal.

We had a fabulous defence that day, there was nobody getting through them. Meath didn't have pace in their full-back line and with Colm gone, there was space so I was able to get free and give our lads an out when we had possession.

What makes the 1989 Munster final special was the atmosphere and the fact we were going down expecting to beat Kerry in Killarney, and then backing that up. Whatever about me thinking that Kerry were finished in 1984, by '89 they were definitely on the ropes.

Their team hadn't evolved and Jack O'Shea and Pat Spillane were still starting for them. Our confidence was up from beating them the two previous years but there was also a feeling that we couldn't lose three All-Irelands in-a-row and so, our focus was on getting to another All-Ireland more than simply beating Kerry.

Kerry had started well but we weathered it, and then Johnno – John O'Driscoll – got a great goal midway through the first-half and we were in control after that.

I was in a set-up that made reaching and winning All-Ireland finals almost an expectation rather than a hope. It was a very good group of footballers and that's something I was proud to be part of.

99

TONY DAVIS
(& DINNY ALLEN)

CORK 0-17 ★ MAYO 1-11
All-Ireland SFC Final
Croke Park
SEPTEMBER 17, 1989

★ **CORK:** J Kerins; N Cahalane, S O'Brien, J Kerrigan; M Slocum, C Counihan, **T Davis**; T McCarthy (0-2), S Fahy; D Barry (0-3), L Tompkins (0-4), B Coffey; P McGrath (0-3), **D Allen**, J Cleary (0-3). **Subs:** J O'Driscoll for Coffey, M McCarthy (0-2) for Fahy, D Culloty for Cleary.

★ **MAYO:** G Irwin; J Browne, P Ford, D Flanagan; M Collins, TJ Kilgallon, J Finn; S Maher, L McHale; G Maher, WJ Padden, D Durkin; M Fitzmaurice, J Bourke, K McStay. **Subs:** A Finnerty for Bourke, R Dempsey for S Maher, B Kilkelly for G Maher.

THE 1989 All-Ireland is very special to me – it was when all the trying came to fruition. It was a relief, but at the same time I never doubted it would happen. The 1990 win is obviously special, with the double and everything else – that'll never again be repeated – but, for me, 1989 is the one. When the final whistle went that day and we won the All-Ireland, it was mission accomplished.

When we were growing up, we played football but we didn't ever really think we'd play with Cork. The competition in West Cork was savage at the time – Castlehaven, Clonakilty, Bantry and Dohenys were all strong – but we didn't really know if we were any good compared to those outside of the region. It was when we went to St Fachtna's and started beating other schools handily – teams that might have had county minor players – that we realised.

That underage competitiveness bore itself out in the 1990s with the county

THE ACTION

★★★★★

WITHOUT THE HISTORY and rancour that Cork and Meath had, the game was open and entertaining. Cork were set on their way with a superb Larry Tompkins free from the right sideline inside the opening minute – it proved to be their only score from a dead-ball, as 16 points from open play followed.

They had four on the board before Willie Joe Padden opened Mayo's account in the 10th minute and, while the Connacht champions did battle back to trail by just 0-6 to 0-5 in the latter part of the first-half, Cork stayed in front as veteran captain Dinny Allen was the satellite around which Dave Barry, John Cleary and Paul McGrath orbited to good effect.

Cork were 0-10 to 0-8 in front at half-time, but the opening stages of the second-half saw Mayo move ahead for the first time. Anthony Finnerty struck for a goal after Cork didn't deal with Liam McHale's delivery.

Conor Counihan came to the fore at centre-back and it was he who set up Barry for the levelling point, before Cleary opened up a two-point lead with a brace of scores. Mayo did come back to level and then go in front again, before Paul McGrath tied the match again, 0-14 to 1-11, and Mayo would not score after that. Sub Mick McCarthy kicked two huge points for Cork, sandwiching one from his namesake Teddy.

★★★★★

football championship. We won in 1992 and lost to the Haven after a replay in the '94 final. Bantry won in 1995, Clon in '96, Beara beat the Haven in '97 and Bantry were back in '98. It was a bit like how the Ulster teams emerged in terms of winning the All-Ireland at the start of the decade.

Cork had been coming. I have a theory that Kerry, because it's so ingrained – and Dublin because of the population – are the only counties that can constantly bring players through. The other counties are relying on a bit of good fortune to have a group of players emerging together. I'm still a big believer in looking after GAA in schools, and making sure they're resourced and keeping people involved as long as you can. The development squads have been fairly successful but fellas identify as Cork players from a young age and that mightn't always be healthy either because, if they don't make it, they're finished.

In Cork, we had that good fortune at the start of the 1980s. The county won three All-Ireland under-21s in-a-row in the early 1980s – I was on the team for the first, in 1984, and then I was captain when we won again in '85. I was born on November 29, 1964, so I was over-age for 1986, when they won again!

We had won the All-Ireland minor in 1981, and that was some team. Mick Maguire was in goal, Niall Cahalane was corner-back, I was wing-back and in the forwards you had John Cleary, Colm O'Neill and Tony O'Sullivan the hurler. Colm O'Neill got three goals in the semi-final against Roscommon, and three more in the final against Derry, but it was Sully gave him the goals! He was a great footballer, he had magic feet.

The minor training used to be up in Carraig na bhFear. Mick Hegarty used to drive us up – we'd leave Fachtna's and in the car you had John Cleary, Mick Burns – God rest him – Niall Cahalane and myself, and we'd pick up Eoin O'Mahony in Clon. What a crowd of lunatics!

It was a long way to go to for Cork training, but I'd have done it in bare feet.

In 1984, I played senior, under-21 and junior for Cork.

A lot of the 1989 and '90 team were on the team that won the junior All-Ireland in '84. It was felt at the time that it would be a good way for us to learn how to play senior football. Basically, anybody that wasn't playing senior club at the time was included – you had Conor Counihan, Teddy McCarthy, Danny

Culloty, Mick McCarthy and a few more.

We had serious craic that year; it was great fun. We played the final against Warwickshire in Coventry – there was a crowd from Skibbereen over there at the time and they nearly kidnapped us the night before the game, we were lucky we were even playing at all!

By that stage, I was a garda in Cork. I came straight out of Templemore and into Union Quay Garda Station – it's not there anymore, since the one on Anglesea St was built. It was handy for Cork training, rather than having to be coming up and down from Skibbereen.

I played in the Centenary Cup that year, too; it was an open-draw competition. In 1985, a similar competition was run, called the Ford Open Cup. We made it to the final but Kerry hammered us, 2-11 to 0-4. There were fellas passing through us and getting goals, and laughing coming out… by Jesus, we banked that.

There was never a fear that we wouldn't translate our underage success to senior. None. That might sound cocky or arrogant, but in our minds, we had won everything underage – minor, under-21, colleges' finals. Looking around, you could see that they were all really good players. Then, once Billy Morgan came along, that was the glue and the knowledge that knitted everything together. It was a perfect storm.

Sports science only really came into Ireland in the last 15 years or so, but Billy was a trained PE teacher. He trained in Strawberry Hill in London, so he had that knowledge and he had a huge interest in other sports. When any of us got a serious injury, we used the FA's Centre of Excellence in Lilleshall. Billy was well before his time, so we were lucky to have him with us. He was able to persuade Dave Barry and Dinny Allen to come back with Cork – someone else wouldn't have had the understanding or the ability to coax them back.

What you had was the best 35 or so players in the county available and all wanting to be involved, and do well. It might seem like an obvious thing but it's not always the case, for whatever circumstance. Billy allowed difference. Difference of opinion and difference of style – he'd allow you on the field to do what you felt was the right thing to do, and back you if it was wrong. He was a special coach.

For an All-Ireland, you'd be going up Saturday on the train and into the Burlington Hotel – and the Burlington would be chaos! The whole of Skibbereen would be there and you'd have fellas up in the room and all sorts, but it was some craic!

I used to always room with Mick McCarthy. We had started primary school together on the same day – there were two Mick McCarthys and the other one was bigger, so that's how the 'Small Mick' nickname came about. We knew each other inside-out but, at the same time, Mick did his own thing… and we all did to an extent – we were comfortable enough with each other to do that.

Billy was open to anything, within reason. The night before a game, sometimes we'd go up to a snooker hall a good bit away from the Burlington. Everybody took football very seriously and nobody was doing the dog, but some lads would have a couple of drinks to settle themselves. I just wanted things to be the same as I'd always done. My ritual was to finish training on a Thursday night, get my gear ready Friday and have it ready to go.

We used to be given shorts and socks by the county board, but I always preferred to wear my own adidas socks. I liked having my socks up anyway and the adidas ones were a small bit elasticated so they stayed up; there was no need to tie them at the top. I wore them for a good while – they were my lucky charm!

There was huge pressure on us; there's no point pretending there wasn't. There was a big emphasis on it because, back then, there wasn't as many other things on. Nowadays, I'd watch all the Munster rugby games, Ireland, the Lions… I'd watch soccer, hurling, the Olympics when it's on – back then, it felt like there was more space in the sporting calendar.

All of the work that had gone before it was made worthwhile by winning an All-Ireland, if that makes sense. You had all this frustration finally being put behind us. The first final against Meath, 1987, was men against boys, really. In 1988, we were ready for them and we should have won it. We would have won it too, but for the free awarded to Meath at the end – it was never a foul, not in a million years – and they made the most of the second chance.

I remember Christmas 1988 – the dinner was nearly ready at home and I went down to Rossa Park for a run. My dad had to come down and look for me because I must have done 50 or 60 laps of the pitch without even knowing it. It was pure madness, thinking of what happened and what we needed to do to win the All-Ireland. It was that kind of an obsession.

But it's worth remembering that the 1989 final against Mayo could have gone west, as well. Anthony Finnerty, who got Mayo's goal, had the ball in his hands and a chance of another and I can still see it in flashbacks. It was a vital stage in the game and if that had gone in, we might have struggled to come back.

There was a big clock up over the Canal End and you were basically looking at it, hoping for the hand to go to five o'clock. It was a game where we were all over them and we should have buried them, but we didn't. Still, all that mattered was getting the win.

It was pure elation but also huge relief. It took over every part of your life, so when that whistle went, it allowed us to relax.

It was lovely to come back to Cork and then to go back home to Skibb. It was a reward for everybody – okay, we were there ourselves, but we were representing our families and the people that looked after us growing up. I always felt that I was never on my own on the pitch – all those people that made sure I was okay at underage, I felt that they were with me.

In 1989, we won the league, the Munster Championship and the All-Ireland – I don't think we even lost a challenge game that year. That was the type of atmosphere that was there. Even the guys on the panel were all good players, who would have been starting for Cork in nearly any other era.

Our whole life was football. Every waking moment, really, but I loved it.

★ ★ ★ ★ ★

DINNY ALLEN

❝

I WAS WONDERING if I was mad, going back in 1988, because coming back doesn't work sometimes. Billy asked me and I was genuinely humming and hawing, wondering if I needed it in my life.

I had played in the Munster final of 1984 down in Killarney; it was a shocking match and we all played terribly. Any one of us could have been dropped after that game, but I was 32 or 33 by that stage so I was one of the obvious fellas to fall first. I was disappointed when I wasn't on the panel when the league came around again for the winter, but at the same time, I was half-glad.

I was thinking that the team didn't look like a force, or anything like that, at that stage and I hadn't played well. Everyone is upset to be dropped and there's no easy way to get out of that, but I half-deserved it, along with other fellas. Then Nemo won the county in 1987 and '88 and that got me back into the limelight, for want of a word.

I played in 1972 in Killarney, when I was still a teenager. We won our first county with Nemo that year too – we beat UCC in the final – but I started playing a bit of soccer as well because the infamous ban was gone. I was approached by St Mary's up on the northside to know if I'd play a few matches with them and I was told, through other guys, that if those games went well, Cork Hibs or Cork Celtic were lingering around the place.

That was my own decision then, and I joined Hibs in January of 1973 and I was missing then until the Munster final of 1975. I didn't pack up soccer; I said that I'd give my preference to the GAA as my friends were in Nemo and with Cork – not that I didn't have friends in soccer, but I was only getting to know them. So, I went back with Cork in 1975 and we had eight Munster finals in-a-row without winning any of them, until '83. The flipside of that is, while it took nine years to win a Munster football final, it took only four months to win a hurling one!

Nemo went senior hurling in 1973; we were there for 10 years and I was having a ball. I nearly enjoyed the hurling more than the football, even though people looked at me as more of a footballer. I played as much hurling growing up as football and it was a breath of fresh air for me that time with Cork and, while Nemo never won a county, we got to two semi-finals. Fellas were asking me at the time, which I preferred, and I probably answered that I liked them both the same but, in reality, I favoured hurling a little bit. The game was a bit fresher and there was less pulling and dragging. There's more to play with when a fella has a hurley in his hand!

The All-Ireland hurling semi-final in 1975 against Galway was a big disappointment. It was a game that we were expected to win, and it was big shock for us to lose, even though they were a good team.

I knew there'd be pressure on me going back in 1988. I was gone now for three-and-a-bit years and, if it didn't turn out well, there'd be egg on my face. Billy asked me; he was obviously involved with Nemo too and he knew what I could do, but I don't think there were too many fellas other than Billy who were calling for me to come back! There was a little bit of thinking that you had something left in you and something to prove.

I did come back and it turned out alright. I got a goal and a couple of points in the Munster final, and I played well. We got to the final against Meath, which was disappointing to lose, but I did alright for myself for the year. I didn't make a fool of myself!

I never played against Meath, in league or championship, until the 1988 All-Ireland. They were never in our section in the league all the time I was there up to 1984. Their style of football was hard to play against and at the time there was no love lost. We wouldn't admit that they were good and they probably wouldn't admit that we were any good, either! History shows that both teams were good.

Ninety-nine times out of a hundred, it wouldn't have worked out the way it did – losing in 1988 and sticking it out another year and becoming captain, and then winning the All-Ireland. It was a freak thing, really.

After 1988, I was saying that that was it, but Billy and the other selectors were pushing me to give it another go, that I still had a lot to contribute to the team. I had been Cork captain in 1976 and again in '82. Tony Nation was captain in 1988 but he was in and out of the team during the National League and I was the oldest Nemo player, so it automatically went to me then – that was the way it was in the club.

We won the league in Dublin – the 'home' final – and went on to New York and the captaincy stuck with me. To beat Dublin in that match in Croke Park gave us fierce belief.

Before the All-Ireland final, the fear of failure was definitely there, but there was none of us talking about it. I remember, as it got close to the match, a group of us – Jimmy Kerrigan, Davie Barry, Barry Coffey, Colman Corrigan – saying that if we didn't the win this time, we wouldn't be able to go back to Cork.

We tried to focus and Billy is an eternal optimist anyway, so he'd have kept us bouncing along. Deep down, we knew that we had to win. There was definitely a fear factor in that regard and in fairness to Mayo, they really put it up to us in the final. At the same time, at that stage and after all the bad results I'd had over the years, I was quite calm about it. When I was playing, friends of mine were nearly more worried about me, than I was about myself. My view was, *I'm playing with Cork and I'm 36, 37 – if we win, we win and if we don't, we don't,* but fellas would say, 'Jesus, you'll have to win it eventually!' I wasn't exactly laid-back about it but I felt that if it was going to happen, it would.

In terms of a pre-match ritual, having two or three pints before an All-Ireland is a good recipe for a sound night's sleep! People nowadays wouldn't drink for three months before an All-Ireland final, but we always had a few and that would be it. It definitely helped to calm you down if you were over-excited.

We were up against it, we were playing a team that was focused, but we were focused, too. Anthony Finnerty got the goal at a great time for Mayo and we might have wavered, but then the second one he shot wide – or so everyone thought! We found out afterwards from John Kerins that he touched that ball out for a '50' and the umpires didn't see it... and John certainly wasn't going to tell them! If he didn't get his fingertip to that, we could be talking about a loss, a third in-a-row.

I was marked by Peter Forde. I didn't score, but my attitude had changed by then. I always liked to think I was able to make scores for fellas, even when I was younger, but the older I got, I knew that I wasn't scoring a lot and Billy knew that as well. I just tried to get it into my head that I had five good forwards around me and I was going to get the ball and look for them, and not worry about scoring or anything like that. That never really worried me anyway because I always seemed to get a few points, club or county.

Those scores weren't coming in the 1989 final, but I didn't mind because the object of the game was to win it. Davy Barry, Larry Tompkins, Paul McGrath, John Cleary – they were great players around me, so all I had to was try to bring them into the game when I got the ball. It was a kind of a simple tactic I had, but it seemed to work. The disappointing thing – maybe 'disappointing' is the wrong word, because we won the match – is that we had very few goal chances. We didn't create them that day, but we still managed to pull away. I think we deserved it.

At the end, it was really relief. Just to get past the finishing post, finally. After playing for 17 or 18 years, there are little men in your head, talking to you. When the final whistle blew, it was total relief. It was a nice feeling that was there for a few weeks, or a month or two.

Fellas involved in the county board and the selectors were saying to me that I surely had something written out for the speech, or even a few bullet points, but I said that I wasn't even going to think about that, because it would have been tempting fate. The speech took care of itself.

We had a good group of fellas and we had got to know each other very well. We had good fun for a couple of weeks afterwards. It's a great memory to have.

I knew that it was the end for me. One or two of the selectors were saying that I'd still have a big influence in the dressing-room if I stayed on, and I might start or whatever, but I cut that decision off at the pass. Billy said not to announce it for two months, that you'd never know what might happen?

I waited, but I knew for every day of those couple of months that there was no chance I'd play again. I had had the perfect finish.

LARRY TOMPKINS

CORK 2-23 ★ KERRY 1-11
Munster SFC Final
Páirc Uí Chaoimh
JULY 1, 1990

★ **CORK:** J Kerins; D Walsh, N Cahalane, S O'Brien; M Slocum (0-1), C Counihan, T Nation; **L Tompkins (0-5)**, D Culloty (1-0); P Hayes (0-1), D Barry (0-3), P McGrath; C O'Neill (0-11), S Fahy (0-2), M McCarthy (1-0). **Sub:** M O'Connor for Counihan.

★ **KERRY:** C Nelligan; S Stack, M Nix, C Murphy; P Slattery, A O'Donovan, T Spillane (0-1); M Fitzgerald (1-5), J Shannon; P Laide (0-1), E Breen, J O'Shea (0-1); S McElligott (0-1), E Liston, S Greaney. **Subs:** P Spillane (0-2) for Shannon, D Farrell for Liston, S Burke for Slattery.

66

NATURALLY, THE 1990 All-Ireland final was special – being captain and beating Meath – but I'd go back slightly to that year's Munster final against Kerry.

Cork won that game by 2-23 to 1-11 and what makes that achievement all the more impressive is that we were without five of the team that had won the 1989 All-Ireland final. We were favourites going in but to back that up and win by such a score was proof of how dominant we had become against Kerry.

People talk about Frank McGuigan kicking 11 points for Tyrone against Armagh in the 1984 Ulster final – Colm O'Neill kicked 11 points for us that day, and nobody ever talks about it! He was putting them over from everywhere that day and I had rarely seen such an exhibition of point-scoring. His input in that game… I'm not saying I had anything to do with it being so important, but I had some influence in Billy picking him.

THE ACTION

★★★★★

NEVER BEFORE HAD Cork beaten Kerry in four straight years; never before had they beaten them by so much.

The win also demonstrated the depth of the Cork panel. Colman Corrigan, Teddy McCarthy, John O'Driscoll and John Cleary were all injured beforehand while Tony Davis and Barry Coffey were named to start, but had to cry off.

In front of 40,065, it did take some time for supremacy to be exerted – four Maurice Fitzgerald frees helped Kerry to lead by 0-5 to 0-4 after 19 minutes, but even then it was clear that Niall Cahalane was well over Eoin Liston at full-back while Cork captain Larry Tompkins dominated midfield.

When he was joined by Shea Fahy, as Danny Culloty switched to full-forward, Cork took control. They had moved in front before Mick McCarthy got the opening goal after a Culloty point attempt came back off the post. Up by 1-6 to 0-5, Cork added five points before half-time as Kerry – forced to bring on Pat Spillane as an early sub – kicked seven wides.

With Cork's defence providing little change, O'Neill and Tompkins were able to ease them clear in the second half. A goal from a penalty by Fitzgerald in the 49th minute was only a brief moment of solace for Kerry, reducing the deficit to 1-15 to 1-8 only for Cork to add six more points without reply.

★★★★★

Jimmy Kerrigan didn't play that day, Teddy McCarthy was out, so were Barry Coffey and John Cleary, while Dinny Allen, who captained us in 1989, had retired. I played midfield with Danny Culloty against Kerry and Shea Fahy was in at full-forward with Dave Barry centre-forward. Paul McGrath was brought out from the corner to the wing… John O'Driscoll was unavailable, so we needed someone who could do a job inside.

Colm was a guy who was a brilliant minor and under-21 player and we all knew he had exceptional talent. We used to train down in Millstreet; Colm would travel with me and every night it was the same conversation, 'What the hell am I doing coming down here?'

It was one of the best games I played for Cork and I used to always slag Colm that he kicked 11 points, but I still ended up as Man of the Match! Colm was such a brilliant footballer and it was great for him to express that talent on that day. I don't think it's highlighted enough. The first free we got that day was one that I could have kicked, but I called Colm out to take it. I was just so delighted for him because, moving forward, he was very significant in terms of us winning the All-Ireland.

Even though Colm was only on the field for 27 or 28 minutes of the All-Ireland final, Mick Lyons used to always say to me that it was the biggest roasting he ever got on the field. I'd rate Mick as one of the best full-backs to ever play the game so, when he says that, you know it means something!

Being captain never really affected me. I was still trying to get the best out of myself and I didn't feel I had to do anything differently. Ever since I had come to Cork in 1987, I was never shy about saying a few words in the dressing-room if I felt they needed to be said. Maybe as I grew into the team, what might have been a two-minute speech in 1987 grew into something longer by '90!

We had Limerick in the Munster semi-final that year, and I didn't play. I had a small bit of trouble with my back and I could have played if I needed to, but Billy wanted me ready for Kerry. I had obviously played a lot of games over the previous few years for club and county and just having that bit of a rest period was a big help. I was down in the Mardyke every morning running and I was never in such good shape as I was before that Munster final. Even so, the word out around the place was that I was struggling to make the match!

I was marking Joe Shannon from Laune Rangers, who was captain of Kerry that year. I can remember Billy telling me that they had earmarked Joe to take me out of it, basically – he only lasted 20 or 25 minutes before being shifted! Maurice Fitzgerald was moved out to mark me then. He was an up-and-coming player and a gifted footballer, but I suppose I was more experienced, and myself and Danny were dominant at midfield that day. Everything was working out for us, basically.

I'm not saying that Billy was wrong but we had gone through 1987, '88, '89 without the team changing much – in fairness, it was a difficult team to change. There was such a hunger there among the fellas trying to break in to the team and that definitely gave us an extra dimension. There's no doubt in my mind that, if we didn't have that, we'd still be waiting to beat Meath. Winning against Kerry like we did really injected lads with confidence.

When you're All-Ireland champions, you need to lay down a marker – and not every team manages to do that. Back in 1990, there was a real sense that we knew that we had unfinished business down the line and Kerry were in the way of that, as much as anything. Add in the fact that the likes of Colm, Mick Slocum, and Danny Culloty were all battling to establish themselves on the team. Mick kicked an incredible point off his left foot in the first-half. When they go over, you know it's going to be your day.

My brother, Martin was sitting beside the great John Corcoran from Ballineen and he made the famous comment as the Kerry fans were leaving early, 'Lock the gates, and make them watch!' To this day, it's a game people talk to me about. Kerry were obviously going through a period of transition but never before did they suffer such a beating!

From start to finish, it was a complete performance against a team that had been hammering Cork over the years. It was nice for the Cork people to get one day out in the sun. It was just special. That performance was a real statement and gave us the bounce to go forward and retain the All-Ireland.

I remember going into the county board meeting a week or two later to present the trophy to the board, as was the tradition. The hurlers were after winning Munster too; Tomás Mulcahy didn't play, so it was Kieran McGuckin alongside me. He had a nice big trophy but the Munster football cup is tiny; I said to the delegates that the only consolation was that, come September, my cup would be a lot bigger – little did we think what lay ahead! Frank Murphy often said it to me about what a good line it was.

When we lost to Kerry in 1991 and '92, people might have thought that that was it for that team, but we came again to win three more Munster titles. In 1993, we could have beaten Derry in the All-Ireland final; fair enough, Down were too good for us in the 1994 semi-final, but '95 against Dublin was a game that could have gone either way.

Even so, we won two All-Irelands… and Cork have only won seven in total. What was so satisfying about that 1990 Munster final was that, as good as the performance was, everybody was ready to go further. Up to this day, if any one of the panel goes into a pub or a restaurant, there's a stature about them, something that comes from winning two All-Irelands. But we wouldn't have had that, if we hadn't beaten Meath. We had to beat Meath and we did

People often ask me if lifting a trophy as Cork captain was less special than it would have been if I was a Kildare captain doing so, and the answer is absolutely not. If this book was about the club Game of my Life, I'd have picked the 1989 county final, when Castlehaven beat St Finbarr's, and that match was what made me Cork captain. Getting such an honour really underlined the acceptance of the Cork people from the word go.

That goes as far back as when we lost the 1987 All-Ireland final, after we came back to the Examiner/Echo offices. I'll never forget it, there were sash windows out on to the veranda on St Patrick's St. Conor Counihan was captain that year and he was outside, speaking to the crowd – there must have been 25,000 people there – and they were chanting for me to come out, too.

The love was always there with Cork people for me, and to accept a cup on their behalf was brilliant.

99

NIALL CAHALANE

CORK 0-11 ★ MEATH 0-9
All-Ireland SFC Final
Croke Park
SEPTEMBER 16, 1990

★ **CORK:** J Kerins; T Nation, S O'Brien, **N Cahalane**; M Slocum, C Counihan, B Coffey; S Fahy (0-4), D Culloty; D Barry, L Tompkins (0-4), T McCarthy; P McGrath (0-1), C O'Neill, M McCarthy (0-2). **Subs:** J O'Driscoll for M McCarthy, P Hayes for Barry, J Cleary for McGrath.

★ **MEATH:** D Smyth; R O'Malley, M Lyons, T Ferguson; B Reilly, K Foley, M O'Connell; L Hayes, G McEntee; D Beggy (0-1), PJ Gillic, C Brady; C O'Rourke, B Stafford (0-6), B Flynn (0-1). **Subs:** C Coyle (0-1) for Brady, J Cassells for McEntee, T Dowd for Beggy.

66

AFTER 1987 AND '88, feeling that we'd left it there – particularly in '88 – in 1989 we were getting wise. We felt we were ready for Meath – and then they didn't come out of Leinster. It was obviously great to win our first All-Ireland; but, beating Mayo at the time, I'm not sure what that had achieved for us as a group. Yes, Cork had won an All-Ireland but we had failed to beat Meath on three occasions, including the drawn game in 1988.

In the 1989-90 National League, we ended up playing them in Croke Park and we were again beaten. It was a semi-final; that year there was a trial rule where the games were split into four quarters. Into the bus, back to the train, down to Cork – it was only a small outing but we were All-Ireland champions and still they turned us over.

I think that, from that evening on, the whole year took a good bit of shape.

THE ACTION

★★★★★

AFTER WINNING MUNSTER, Cork had got past Roscommon in the All-Ireland semi-final while Meath impressed as they saw off Donegal. Then, Cork claimed the All-Ireland hurling title – expectations soared on Leeside.

With Shea Fahy and Danny Culloty gaining the early upper-hand at midfield, Cork enjoyed a good start and might have had a goal from Colm O'Neill, whose shot came back off the crossbar. Meath rallied to tie the game at 0-3 each but it would prove to be the only time the sides were level.

Two points from the lively Mick McCarthy and other from Fahy had Cork 0-6 to 0-4 in front before a potentially pivotal moment. O'Neill and Meath full-back Mick Lyons had both been booked after an early skirmish and O'Neill was sent off after they again became entangled shortly before half-time.

Brian Stafford pointed just before the interval, resulting in Cork going in a point up but having to play the second-half a player down. Meath failed to make the most of their manpower though and Fahy launched another booming point after the restart, followed by one from Paul McGrath.

While impressive sub Colm Coyle and David Beggy scored to bring Meath back to within a point, 0-8 to 0-7, with 20 minutes left. They couldn't level though and Larry Tompkins' free gave breathing room to Cork. Fahy kicked his fourth point before another Tompkins free, and the lead was four points by the 59th minute. The double was almost done.

★★★★★

If we had beaten Meath, maybe we'd have taken things a bit for granted. I can remember going back to training on the Tuesday night and you could feel the hurt from having been beaten again, even if it was only the league.

We became very focused – managers, players, everyone involved – on getting to Croke Park in September again and hoping that Meath were good enough to come through the other side.

It was Easter Sunday that we lost to Meath, and the following day the hurlers were tarred by Wexford in a league semi-final. They turned their year around, came out of nowhere and won the All-Ireland. That meant that, for the next two weeks, we were trying to go about our bit of business and it was just manic. Did it pile on a lot of extra pressure? Yes, it had to. We'd have been way better off if they hadn't won, and we'd have been coming in under the radar a bit.

That whole fortnight was just crazy and expectations with the general public were sky-high. We didn't need that in our lives, but I will credit management with the fact that we never lost focus with our job at hand. It couldn't have been easy at the time to keep the whole thing grounded and keep it on course.

That time, being a corner-back in Croke Park could be a fairly lonely existence if your corner-forward stood out by the corner flag... and could do the 100 metres in 11 seconds. It's probably much more scientific and streamlined now – I watch games and I think that it's probably much more fun being a defender. You're getting on more ball anyway and you've more fellas to cover you... it's very rare that you're clean exposed in a one-on-one.

Being a defender was challenging and you had to look after yourself. You had to perfect your tackle... you had to perfect different things because, invariably, in any given game, the corner-forward, full-forward or wing-forward was going to get half-a-dozen opportunities to take you on.

We were lucky that we had Frank Cogan to do a lot of work with the backs, having been a defender himself. I'll ever remember Frank saying that you certainly could leave your man out from you, but you certainly couldn't leave him in beyond you. You didn't have the zone defences and it was man-on-man.

I was okay at that. A lot of people might have said that I was caught for a little bit of pace, from A to B – but I remember once reading an article about one of the German soccer defenders and the same question was to put him; he said he never started at A! It was all about positioning yourself, and timing and anticipation.

Did I play on the edge? If you didn't, you were wasting your time. There was a bit of fun in that as well – it was a challenge and it didn't always go right for me. But a lot of times it did!

Was it enjoyable being a defender? Sure, it had to be more enjoyable being a forward or a midfielder. It was certainly a challenge but, when you got results and did okay, you had a lot of satisfaction.

The great thing about Castlehaven was that they had no problem playing 17- or 18-year-olds at senior level if they were good enough. The Barrs had it over us at the time – ever so slightly, and they were winning All-Irelands. I can remember playing them as a teenager and they'd have Cork under-21s that couldn't get on their team. We got a great grounding from that point of view.

I was fortunate that there was a very good crop of Haven players emerging at around the same time – apart from myself, there was John and Denis Cleary, Mick Burns, Michael Maguire, and Brian Collins. I was also fortunate that Cork were strong – we won the All-Ireland minor in 1981, and the under-21 in 1984. In 1982, we lost to Roscommon in the All-Ireland semi-final with a last-minute goal and in '83 Kerry beat us by a point down in Castleisland.

In 1984, there were a lot of the under-21s on the senior panel but the cut-off for match-day squads was 21 players and that was disappointing – after working so hard, you couldn't tog for the big match.

I was 10 when Castlehaven won their first West Cork junior A divisional title in 1973. Three years later, they won it again and won a county junior. All of those fellas were our role models. From a Cork point of view, would I have looked at a defender as the one to base myself on? No, I'd have always said that Jimmy Barry-Murphy was the one – he wasn't that much older but he was just someone who you felt had it all.

He was this fella that came along at 18 and set the whole world alight. From a football point of view, it was a shame that, halfway through his career, he retired and focused fully on hurling. I think football in Cork was probably the worse for it.

Of course, nowadays my sons, Damien and Conor are on the Cork hurling panel. Hurling has always been more popular in Cork; maybe it's a more fun thing, I don't know. I was never going to dictate to them what they should play – the girls didn't really have an opportunity to play soccer growing up, but the lads all played with Greenwood, up to around under-17 or so.

Damien actually won a national cup at under-16 level in 2009, on the same team as John Egan – Damien was in goal and actually scored from a kickout. He was meant to go over to Sunderland for a trial at the same time as John, but St Finbarr's had a county hurling semi-final against Newtownshandrum the same weekend and didn't go. With these things, you're not asked again.

I played a bit of hurling myself, with Blackrock.

Castlehaven actually played hurling once upon a time – we won West Cork B titles at under-16 and under-21. The club went senior in football after 1978 and even won the West Cork Junior B hurling in 1980, but soon after that it was said at an AGM that there was no way they would have become successful in both… and so the hurling side of it was scrapped.

I obviously had an interest in Blackrock, because Donie and Francis Collins were playing for them. My father used to bring us to all of their games but I didn't know anyone else in the club. We got great satisfaction out of them doing well – we'd come home from county finals thinking we were hurlers ourselves!

In 1986, I was on the Ireland panel for the compromise rules in Australia and we were out there while the county hurling final was on here – Blackrock were playing Midleton. There were no mobile phones at the time and I was in the hotel, going to the public phone to ring home and find out what the latest score was? Frank Murphy was out there with us and, at one stage, I was heading for the phone and so was he. He was curious as to why I was interested in it and I explained. He asked if I'd be interested in playing hurling again, and I said that I'd love to. I went down there for 1987, thinking I'd be playing a bit of junior hurling and, the next thing, I was on the senior team! Donie Collins had gone to Kilkenny by that stage but I got to play with Francis, which was great.

Now, I was f**king hopeless at it, I'd be the first to admit that! I wasn't a hurler, but I enjoyed the few years I had there.

I wore No 3 in the 1990 final, but I was always going to play left corner-back.

When a big game was coming up, it was always nice to know a little bit in advance who you would be picking up because you could go away and do a small bit of research. By the time we had beaten Roscommon in the semi-final and Meath had come through the other side, I knew I was going to be picking up Colm O'Rourke.

I hadn't marked him in any of the previous meetings – I had picked him up at stages but I was never properly sent out to shadow him. My thinking was that he was probably their go-to man when it came to putting big scores up, so I had to limit him as best I could. I felt that, if I could, it would go some way towards helping us.

Leading up to the game, I would have been so confident that we were going to win. The only hiccup was that we lost Colm O'Neill, which was a bit of a ball-breaker. One consolation of sorts was that it's probably easier to cope with losing a forward rather than having a back sent off and needing to rejig your defence. For those few years, our defence was fairly nailed down… Steven O'Brien was the only real addition, after Colman Corrigan's injury. There might be the odd positional change but it was the same group of seven or eight defenders across that time and there was a fierce understanding.

I've seven Munster senior football medals, which, looking back at it, was marvellous. Then, you see that they converted into two All-Irelands, and there was one National League win – should it have been more?

It was competitive – beyond Meath, Dublin were strong and Roscommon and Galway were hanging around the place at the time. Then the Ulster explosion happened in the early 1990s. Back then, there was always a day when you could go out and get beaten by a minnow; there was always that element of surprise, whereas that's not there now.

You look at the history of Cork football and, unlike the hurlers, they have never been the standard-bearers. They have come and made a bit of a hit, and disappeared again. You look at the All-Ireland wins – 1890, 1911, 1945, 1973, 1989, 1990 and 2010 – and we could be waiting another while again. Because there has been such a wait since the last hurling win, the football gap gets completely overlooked.

I was captain of the last Cork team to beat Kerry in Killarney, which was back in 1995, a hell of a long time ago. I wasn't young then, but I felt that we the ability to turn Kerry over a couple of more times in Killarney, but it hasn't happened since. That eight-to-10-year period we had was probably our golden years, contesting five All-Irelands and a replay.

The last championship match I played for Cork was the 1996 Munster final loss against Kerry in Páirc Uí Chaoimh. I played midfield alongside Liam Honohan – the only year I played there for Cork – and I kicked a point. The last time I togged out for Cork was against Clare in Ennis in 1997.

I had broken my cheekbone maybe three weeks previously but I was still available for selection and, having been on the team for years, it was a bit of a surprise not to be picked. I was doing a small bit of stretching and Damien – who was only four at the time and used to tag along to training – came up and asked me what was wrong. I said, 'You won't believe it, I'm not starting!' I was having an adult conversation with a kid.

Damien replied, 'You must be starting… sure Larry's our friend!'

Don't get me wrong, it isn't something I was sour about afterwards, but at the time you're thinking, *Did I really have to wait for this to happen?* You have all of these things going on in your head.

We were up in Ennis on the Sunday and the game was very close. I was sitting next to Dr Con Murphy in the dug-out and, if you needed a shoulder to cry on, Con was the man. I asked him at what stage they were going to throw me in and he said, 'Well, you have to wait now for a fortnight, because they've brought on the three subs'.

'Ah Jesus!' I shouted.

But Con replied, 'All we have to do now is hang on here and you can have any position you want for the Munster final, because there's no-one shooting the lights out.'

Clare got a free in injury time… and I could see this happening in front of my eyes. I was nearly inside the white line at this stage; all I wanted to do was clock someone, stop the game, give us a big dust-up… and we'd settle down and win by two points.

We lacked the experience on the pitch to do that – we were innocent. Had we only been a point up, Martin Daly would have gone for a point rather than a goal and we'd have gone to a replay – and I'd have probably got my place for that.

I'd like to think that I couldn't have given anymore to Cork football.

Maybe I could – maybe I could have perfected things a little bit better, I'm not too sure. When I see the way teams prepare nowadays and what goes into it, you'd often wonder could you have? At the time, I don't think I could have given it an awful lot more.

It was marvellous to go to Killarney and play in front of 50,000 on a day when you could fry an egg on the road on the way in. Going up O'Connell St on the bus on All-Ireland final day and seeing the Cork crowd? The after-match celebrations. It was all brilliant.

Did I enjoy my career? Of course, but I think it was more satisfaction – not personal, but that Cork or Castlehaven were doing well and I was a part of it.

JOE KAVANAGH

CORK 1-10 ★ KERRY 0-10
Munster SFC Semi-Final
Fitzgerald Stadium
JUNE 20, 1993

★ **CORK:** J Kerins; M Farr, M O'Connor, N Cahalane; C O'Sullivan, S O'Brien, T Davis; S Fahy, T McCarthy; D Davis, L Tompkins (0-1), B Coffey; C Corkery (0-6), **J Kavanagh (1-2)**, J Cleary (0-1). **Sub:** L Honohan for Coffey.

★ **KERRY:** P O'Leary; C Murphy, K Culhane, M Nix; S Moynihan, S Burke, L O'Flaherty; D Hanafin (0-1), B McElligott; M Fitzgerald (0-7), E Breen (0-1), T Fleming; B O'Shea, E Liston, K O'Dwyer (0-1). **Subs:** N O'Mahony for McElligott, C Kearney for Liston, P Dennehy for Murphy.

"

HERE I WAS my first trip to Killarney as a senior player and I was going with the guys that I had been going to Killarney to see playing… Tompkins, Cahalane, O'Brien. That's why it sticks out, and obviously the fact we won was a help! As it turned out, it's still Cork's second-last victory down there.

I was just out of minor and Billy Morgan invited me down to training in the Páirc. It was huge at the time for me, I wasn't expecting it at all.

We had won the minor All-Ireland in 1991 and a few lads from that team were called in. For a young fella, for Billy to ask me personally like that, I was delighted. I can remember one of my first sessions with the panel and we were running around the tunnel at the old Páirc. I wasn't used to senior training and this was a very physical session – I was feeling a bit dizzy and felt I was going to get sick, which I did!

THE ACTION

★★★★★

AFTER THE 1990 dismantling of Kerry, Cork didn't face their neighbours in a Munster final until 1995.

However, Kerry failed to win the provincial title in 1992, though, losing to Clare, and Billy Morgan's team got back on top in 1993. This was a semi-final – the first time Kerry did not reach a Munster final since 1957 – and Cork would go on to beat Tipperary in the final. The team that had reached four All-Ireland deciders was evolving and seven of the side to receive game-time in Killarney would go on to win maiden Munster medals.

Cork, with Ciarán O'Sullivan, Steven O'Brien and Tony Davis excellent in the half-back line, and Teddy McCarthy imperious at midfield, led by 0-5 to 0-4 at half-time but only because some great goal opportunities were passed up – Kerry goalkeeper Peter O'Leary made two good saves while Morgan Nix denied Barry Coffey and Joe Kavanagh shot narrowly wide.

Kavanagh, playing against Kerry for the first time, was a constant threat and he got his reward close to the end as another newcomer, his Nemo Rangers clubmate, Colin Corkery, and Larry Tompkins combined to fashion an opening. Kavanagh slotted past O'Leary and, while two late Kerry points cut the gap – all but one of their scores to that point were Maurice Fitzgerald frees.

Unfortunately, there was not to be another All-Ireland – Derry defeated Cork in September – but they were back on top in Munster.

★★★★★

I presumed after that, that I could tog in and have a shower. I was just after getting a drink of water and I could hear Billy's voice shouting, 'Where the f**k is Kavanagh?!' I told him I got sick and he just said to get back up with the rest, so I knew then that that there'd be no favouritism or anything, even though I was from Nemo. I wouldn't say I was awe-struck going into the dressing-room but these were household names. A few years previously, I had been going to watch them as a 14- or 15-year-old and now here I was playing with them. It was a case of wanting to be in that group and wanting to be part of it – thinking that you're going to carry on what they had done from 1987-90.

I wanted to be Tony Nation, and I wanted to be Dinny Allen… and now, I was actually with them, so I wanted to stay in that group and see where it brought me. The years that followed brought me some great memories but sadly they didn't bring any All-Ireland!

I played my first game in the league in 1992 – my debut was against Dublin and I scored 2-3. I can't remember if I played a second or third game before we played championship. We had Kerry in the first round and we were beaten, so it was like, Welcome to it, but you're gone again. The speed of it and the physicality were the biggest noticeable differences, which is hardly surprising. There was serious pulling and dragging going on back then and off-the-ball stuff… you had to man up before you were a man, as such! Essentially, you just got accustomed to it and never gave out about it, it was just a matter of getting on with it.

Getting a good night's sleep was always very important to me and then making sure the boots were in pristine condition. That was one thing I always would have done – washed them and polished them, and kept them in good shape.

It was always adidas boots I wore because when I came in first I was given two pairs of them. We were always well looked after in terms of gear – I can remember bringing home bags of stuff and my brothers were delighted!

That was my first time going to Killarney for a game and playing in front of a big crowd. The whole thing about being a Cork senior, meeting in the morning and getting a bus down and heading to the hotel beforehand – the crowd can see you approaching and there's a great atmosphere. All that added to it, especially for a 19-year-old. Then you're going through the town, heading to the stadium and there's thousands of people outside the bars, soaking up the atmosphere. I had been among those crowds – not drinking, obviously! – but it's those memories that really make it stick in my head.

Centre-forward was where I played most of my football and I loved it – you could spray the ball around and that's what I felt I was good at – but previous to that I was full-forward a lot for Cork minors and under-21s. I had been centre-forward against Clare in the Munster semi-final in 1993, but Larry Tompkins was back for the Kerry match and he was No 11 so I moved to 14. When you're getting good ball, full-forward is the best place in the world; on the other hand, if the ball's not coming in, it's not a lot of fun! Coming from centre-forward, you still got the opportunity to go for goals like a full-forward.

In terms of the game itself, my main memories are a couple of goal chances that Peter O'Keeffe denied me in the first-half. Then in the second-half I scored the 'soccer goal' that everyone remembers and the celebration after it was more from relief on my side that I was after eventually getting one, because your man had already made two great saves. The goal I did score, I drew him out and then it was the best thing to just roll it past him.

The year ended on a disappointing note; obviously it's well-documented that we lost to Derry in the final and Tony Davis was sent off, unfairly. Would a 15-man Cork team have beaten a 15-man Derry team? We'd have liked to think so. It would have been the medal in the pocket and then see where we went from there. I can remember people saying to me, 'You're young, you've got years ahead of you', but then the years came and went very quickly! It would have been good to have it done young, and whatever happened after that would have happened.

The fact that Derek won a medal in 2010 was great for the family and it's still hanging up in the home place with a picture of him holding the cup and the parents alongside him. Personally speaking, the physical medals I've won, I don't know where they are – probably in the attic! – but when someone asks what you've won, you know the figures about what you've done.

The flipside is that you know what you didn't do, what you lost.

I'd obviously liked to have won one – when people ask about playing with Cork, the next question is whether I won an All-Ireland? – but I've no major regrets. You can't do anything about it at this stage!

CIARÁN O'SULLIVAN
(& KEVIN O'DWYER)

CORK 0-15 ★ KERRY 1-9
Munster SFC Final
Fitzgerald Stadium
JULY 23, 1995

★ **CORK: K O'Dwyer**; M Farr, M O'Connor, N Cahalane (0-1); **C O'Sullivan (0-2)**, S O'Brien, B Corcoran; D Culloty, L Honohan; D Davis (0-3), J Kavanagh (0-1), P O'Mahony; S Calnan, L Tompkins, C Corkery (0-7). **Subs:** M O'Sullivan (0-1) for Calnan, T McCarthy for Tompkins, J O'Driscoll for O'Mahony

★ **KERRY:** P O'Brien; M Hassett (0-1), S Burke, M Nix; D Ó Cinnéide, S Moynihan, E Breen (1-0); C Kearney, L O'Flaherty; B O'Driscoll (0-1), L Hassett, J Crowley; B O'Shea, M Fitzgerald (0-4), G Farrell (0-2). **Subs:** P Dennehy (0-1) for Crowley, D Ó Sé for Kearney, A Gleeson for M Hassett.

66

I ALWAYS LOVED playing in Killarney. There's something special about the place – the crowd were right in on top of you, and the atmosphere was super.

It used to be a really special weekend for people, especially if you were coming away with a win. We did that in 1995, but I don't think anyone thought we'd still be waiting in 2023 for the next one there.

I went to boarding school, Coláiste Íosagáin in Baile Bhúirne for five years, and we had Paudie Herlihy and Mickey 'Ned' O'Sullivan coaching us, which was a good start!

Historically, there would have been a good tradition of Beara lads going there – at one stage, before my time, a bus used to bring them back on the Sunday evenings. It used to be a teacher-training school and even after that, it was still a stepping-stone towards becoming a teacher.

THE ACTION

★★★★★

THERE WAS NOTHING too out of the ordinary as Cork captain Niall Cahalane lifted the Munster senior football cup – certainly nothing to suggest that, nearly 30 years later, the Rebels would be waiting for their next win there.

This victory for Billy Morgan's side was the fourth time in five visits that Cork had emerged victorious and it represented the third consecutive provincial title for the Rebels, a seventh in nine years. Kerry had gained some early hope. There were less than two minutes on the clock when Maurice Fitzgerald waltzed through the Cork defence and was able to place wing-back Eamonn Breen for an easy close-range finish to the net.

The goal would help to keep Kerry well in contention – they even led coming up to half-time – but Cork were getting on top and Joe Kavanagh, Don Davis and Colin Corkery (free) got the last scores of the first-half to leave matters tied, 1-4 to 0-7, at the interval.

Fitzgerald and Gene Farrell got the first two scores of the second half for Kerry and it was 1-8 to 0-9 after 52 minutes but the home side would concede six unanswered points as Cork finally fully asserted themselves.

Larry Tompkins set Davis up for a point to cut the gap to one and then Corkery put Cork ahead once more with a free, and then a sideline kick.

★★★★★

The college had won the Corn na Mumhan seven times but, by the time I was finishing, it was in the process of closing down and the numbers were dwindling as there were no new students coming in. For the 1987-88 academic year – the year I left – we participated in the vocational schools' competitions and won the All-Ireland. We beat Dungannon of Tyrone in the final, which was on in Croke Park before the National League final. Peter Keane, who would go on to manage Kerry, was corner-forward on that team.

Íosagáin was a very strong GAA-playing school but basketball was a very close number two and, to me, the two complemented each other. John O'Driscoll from Ballingeary went there as well – he was a few years ahead of me – and he played basketball for Ireland; so did Aindrias Ó Súilleabháin, who was midfield with me that day in Croke Park.

As well as winning the All-Ireland, I was picked on the Cork Vocational Schools' team that year and then I got on the Cork minor team. Unfortunately, we were beaten by Kerry by a point in 1988 and that set a pattern. In 1990, when I was on the under-21 panel but not playing, we lost to them below in Tralee. My final year under-21, I was midfield and Kerry beat us in Páirc Uí Chaoimh on a ferocious night – the game should never have gone ahead, the pitch was in muck.

I did however win an All-Ireland junior medal in 1990; we beat Warwickshire in the final in Páirc Uí Chaoimh. I was playing with guys that had good experience – John Caulfield, who was playing for Cork City at the time, was playing and he was as cute as a fox inside in the full-forward line. Mark Farr and Paul Coleman were on that team and would go on to play senior later in the decade – and Colm O'Neill and Paddy Hayes actually played in the Munster final win over Kerry in June before going on to feature in the All-Ireland senior final.

In 1991, I was in and out of training with the seniors but I wasn't a part of any match-day squad. I was more involved in 1992 and would have played some league games. Urhan won the junior county that year after three famous days against Midleton below in Ballingeary, so that was another stepping stone.

If you'd told me then that I'd be playing in the All-Ireland senior final a year later, I'd have loved it, but I mightn't have believed it! All I wanted do at the time was just be a part of it and claim a position, if I could. With the school and the club, I was always a midfielder but, when I came in to Cork first, I was playing as a wing-forward. I'll always put the success of my switch to wing-back down to Billy Morgan – I couldn't say enough good about him as a manager, he was unbelievable.

My last game as a wing-forward was above in Kildare. I felt I was going okay – I kicked a point in the first-half – but I was taken off at half-time. I said to myself, This is it, this doesn't look good, but I got a phone call from Billy the next day… and that's the type of manager he was. He told me to keep the head up, keep working, and something would happen for me.

We went to open a pitch with Cork. I think it was in Aughrim, in Wicklow, and we were staying overnight as we had a game arranged the next day too, but where that was, I've no idea. He handed me the No 5 jersey in the dressing-room before the game and I was thinking, *Oh my God, here goes!* And I hardly ever took it off again. I really enjoyed the role. Obviously, I had to defend but I loved being able to drive forward as opposed to having to turn and go back. Of course, you were still up against the likes of Anthony Davis and Mick Slocum and these fellas, which was quite a challenge.

When I came in to a dressing-room full of fellas with All-Ireland medals, I tried not to take any notice – I just put my head down and worked hard. I respected them unbelievably because you had the likes of Teddy McCarthy, John Kerins and Mick McCarthy, God rest them, Niall Cahalane, Conor Counihan, John Cleary, Danny Culloty – you had all these lads and I was a young garsún coming in, but there were a few others. Don Davis, Colin Corkery and Joe Kavanagh, we all came in around the same time… and Mark O'Connor wasn't too much ahead of us.

Billy had a great way of getting the best of you and you always knew that he had your back. He would tell you something straight out – it mightn't be what you'd want to hear at times, but that was his way. He'd be very honest, very open and he'd back you to the hilt. That's the way he was and is, so players had savage respect for him. He never plámásed you; if he had something to say, he'd say it.

He was fiery, we all knew that; but if he did lose it and say something, 30 seconds later that was gone. He'd always be the first man to fight for you.

That first year that I was regular, 1993, we made it to the All-Ireland final but we lost to Derry. I'll never forget it, the crowd started to come on the field and I ran off with John Kerins – he went straight for the corner of the Canal End and the

Hogan Stand, where the old dressing-rooms used to be, and I shot off after him. I was devastated, obviously, but I would have met people that night and over the next few weeks who all said, 'Don't worry about it Ciarán, you've plenty of time ahead of you'. It doesn't work that way, obviously.

You just have to get back on with it – I tried, but I did my cruciate the following year, in an intermediate championship match for Urhan against the Barrs, about three weeks or a month before the Munster final. It was frustrating, of course, but I had no choice only to accept it and I worked exceptionally hard to come back again.

I was lucky in that everything went right and I was back training after six months. I went over to Lilleshall for a week for rehabilitation, which Cork County Board paid for. The late Dan Hoare was treasurer at the time; what a gentleman he was. During my rehab, I used to be up and down to the gym in Páirc Uí Chaoimh and the late Tommy Lynch looked after me – he would have the showers ready and the ice-packs. Tommy was unbelievable... oh my God, what a legend.

The fact that I bounced back was part of the reason for the 1995 Munster final being so special. Of course, Killarney was close enough to us down in Beara anyway and I used to nearly find it more enjoyable playing there than in Páirc Uí Chaoimh.

We stayed the night that year in the Castlerosse Hotel – other years, the team would travel on the day and, after I moved back to Urhan, I used to make my own way to Killarney. Staying the night allowed us to be together in the morning and plan for the game. I liked to keep my own preparations fairly straightforward; once I had all my gear in my bag, I was ready to go.

I think it was Billy O'Shea I was marking in 1995. As a wing-back, you were going out to mark a fella but you were trying to put your man on the back foot to a certain degree and have him chasing you. At the same time, you had to be conscious that Kerry were dangerous. They had some good forwards and the priority was obviously to defend but, any opportunity that opened up, you were encouraged to drive forward.

Even though we got a bad start on the day – they got a goal straightaway and we were under pressure – we got on top and we really finished strongly. I kicked two points that day; Don kicked three and I was slagging him that he kicked more that day than he did all year! It was a savage occasion and nip-and-tuck throughout the game. We really pushed on at the end to get the win and, any few Kerry lads that were still hanging on at that stage, it was the final nail for them.

For me, it was a really memorable one.

I can't really believe that it's still Cork's last win there. I've been at many a game there since, supporting Cork, and we've drawn there numerous times, including 2002, when I was still playing. We had a great chance in 2015, when I was a selector under Brian Cuthbert – time was up and Fionn Fitzgerald, the Kerry corner-back, kicked a huge point to level it. Prior to that, Conor Counihan's team went close a couple of times, but Colm Cooper scored equalising frees – and, without sounding biased, those frees might have been a bit dubious!

I wasn't involved in 2003, but Billy brought me back in '04 and my last game was the defeat to Fermanagh in Croke Park in 2004. Does it bother me that I didn't win an All-Ireland with Cork? Hand on my heart, I would have no regrets whatsoever.

At the time, you were gutted to lose two All-Irelands, of course you were – maybe more so in 1999 than '93. Number one, I probably felt that we had a better chance of beating Meath, and also, I was 29 years of age at the time and getting ready to move home. I knew that, from then on, it was going to become more challenging to be travelling up from Beara, though I still did it for a few more years.

It's not something that stops me from going to sleep at night. I consider myself blessed to have met so many super people through football, the best of friends – within Cork and outside of the county too, Kerry and everywhere else. I was lucky enough that I travelled to Australia in 1999, with Joe, to play International Rules.

We got a pile out of it and made friends for life.

★ ★ ★ ★ ★

KEVIN O'DWYER

66

IT WAS BR PATRICK Kelly who made me a goalkeeper when I was first year in St Fachtna's. I was the same size then as I am now and we didn't have a 'keeper so he threw me in. I ended up playing there as Skibb beat Douglas in a county under-14 final and that was the end of it!

Br Patrick was from Kerry – a brother of the future GAA president, Seán – and sadly he died only a few years later, but he was mad for football and turned Fachtna's around. John Brady came in after that and we won the Corn Uí Mhuirí when I was in Fifth Year and again in Sixth Year, when we went on to win the All-Ireland, the Hogan Cup. That was 1991 and we're the last Cork school to win it.

Noel Crowley had thrown me in goal for the Skibb seniors in 1990. We were playing Glanmire in the first game of a double-header in Bandon – Castlehaven and Muskerry were on after us. I was only 16 but Noel took a chance on me. I saved a penalty from Teddy McCarthy that day; they scored the rebound, but we still won well. I did well enough and Pat O'Donovan from Bantry, God rest him, was at the game coming out and he told me to link up with the Cork minor panel.

After that, I ended up being the Cork minor goalkeeper for two years, and we won the All-Ireland in 1991. Then Skibb won the county championship in 1992 – we would go on to win the Munster and All-Ireland – and a good few of us were given a chance with Cork. We went up to Dublin to play that great Down team in a challenge match at St Vincent's. No doubt, I was an arrogant little fella and I'll always remember, Mickey Linden scored two goals – the ball had flashed past me before I'd even moved.

He made a small boy out of me and I hopped on the bus afterwards, thinking, *I'm out of my depth here at the moment!* Up to then, everything had just come naturally… and now there was a realisation that I was going to have to take things to a whole extra level.

I wouldn't say I was the most natural of goalkeepers – I'm not six-foot-four or anything. I realised I was going to have to work damn hard to get anywhere near the standards required. Now, I was still only 18 or 19 and playing inter-county football was a big deal, but that Down game just brought it home that it was a huge step up.

It was a valuable lesson, in hindsight. Billy arranged for me to train with Cork City and College Corinthians, doing specialised training during the winter. I looked for it and Billy provided it thanks to his contacts; he was always good at facilitating things. Corinthians had a sandpit for goalkeeping work, so you weren't landing on hard ground all the time. The guy doing the goalkeeper coaching was Gerry McEneaney, who was in the army – he's now the President of the FAI!

Now, I enjoyed my time off, but I just knew that I had to work very hard. As someone who wasn't a natural goalkeeper, I had to get physically very fit every year, to do the amount of goalkeeping training that I had to do. Now, maybe I overdid it, to the point that they were more like stamina sessions. It'd be way different now, but back then you just had to do a lot of work that nobody saw. In Cullen, where I had moved after becoming a garda, there's a ball alley and it was a case of hours, hours… hours there.

You couldn't pull the wool over Billy's eyes. I'll always remember a game – this was later on, in his second stint – we were playing in Páirc Uí Rinn around February or March in the rain and I made two or three good saves in the first-half, but I had sliced two kickouts. Badly. I was strolling away in, happy enough with myself, but he went through me for a shortcut.

Also in the background, and he doesn't get the credit that he deserved, was Frank Cogan. He used to take the backs, and he was massive in terms of reading the game and situations and stuff like that. He did a lot of defensive work, where I was to be to support players and that kind of thing. Between himself and Billy, they'd keep a goalkeeper on his toes!

The reason I can pinpoint my league debut as December 1992 was because it came after O'Donovan Rossa had won the county title – there were eight Skibbereen fellas playing against Donegal that day. It was a great start. Mick was a genius, and Don was one of these annoying fellas that would come back in February and, after 10 minutes of doing runs, he'd be fit.

Anthony always drove the standards. He was a perfectionist, always looked after himself, and I took a lot from him. He always minded me up there; he was a rock, really. Myself and Don were garsúns but Anthony had been there and done that, and built up the experience. There were other great footballers there but, for the first few years, Anthony was the go-to guy.

Like any goalkeeper, I made my fair share of mistakes – but I was lucky in that, usually, when I did make one, we still won the game! I had a fight with the crossbar in 2002 in the replay against Kerry – the goalkeeper isn't going to win that! I made a bad mistake against Galway in 2005 in Croke Park; I came out and lost the flight of the ball but we won a great game, which allowed the opportunity to bounce back in the next game.

I don't say that I wouldn't have let mistakes bother me, but I'd always have been a good fella to analyse a goal after it was scored and what I did wrong – I'd be doing this even while the game was going on, just in case something else would come up again. I'd always bank a lot of knowledge from games and against different opponents and so on. I was there for 12 years and there were plenty of goalkeepers who came through the panels and a few of them used to let the mistakes get to them. Br Patrick used to say that, in my case, it was more stupidity than anything else, but it just didn't bother me! I never dropped the head and always made sure I had someone else to blame!

That was how I felt about the Munster final in 1995. My view was, *I'm here now and whatever happens, barring a Paddy Cullen moment, they can't take it away from me. If I make a balls of it and I'm dropped, at least I made it here.*

John Kerins retired after Cork lost to Down in the All-Ireland semi-final in 1994. We'd be training before Christmas and there were legendary sessions down below in Páirc Uí Chaoimh. Now, we had our craic after, but you were talking three-hour sessions with Billy and you never got a chance to relax.

I'd always be putting myself under pressure but I wouldn't think I was under pressure from somebody else. I couldn't control what anyone else would do, but it just sort of rolled seamlessly. I can't remember really doubting that I would make the team – is that the arrogance of youth, maybe? My first game was in December 1992 and I would have had credit in the bank from 1993 and '94, a trust built up. I was definitely a hard worker and he'd always appreciate that. Even so, the team would be called out after training, above in the boardroom in Páirc Uí Chaoimh, and you would be a small bit nervous, waiting for your name.

That time, you were always focused on Kerry. I couldn't even remember without checking who else we played in the Munster Championship in a given year. It was straight knockout, you were back before Christmas for the start of the league and the Kerry game would be June or July… so you were training for eight or nine months essentially for one game. You weren't even talking All-Irelands, it was just Kerry. Games against anyone else were just opportunities to get yourself dropped!

Tipperary had great footballers coming on and we got caught by Clare later on. Maybe it was just the arrogance of the time, coming from the late 1980s into the 90s, but it was just Cork and Kerry, either in the Páirc or in Killarney, and that was the focus.

I'd always be second out on to the pitch after the captain, but that was just a habit more than anything else. On one occasion, I was second out behind Niall Cahalane for a game in the Páirc – it must have been 1995 as he was captain that year. Back then, there were railings in front of the entrance to the tunnel and Cahalane went straight out and jumped over them. I had one look and thought, *Nah*, and went around it!

Coming up to a big game, I'd have no problems walking around town and talking to people. Now, the day before a game, I'd go to ground and spend it on the couch, just relaxing. Now, you couldn't get it out of your head because it was the biggest day of the GAA calendar for us. The Munster hurling and football finals were huge events that time.

Every sort of scenario, I'd run through – bad and good, like dropping a ball or whatever. Maybe that helped me when bad things happened, as I'd have thought about them the day before – *What if this happens, what if they get a penalty, what if you miskick the ball, what if you drop the ball?* That, if you saved a penalty, you wouldn't get too excited. I suppose now they call it visualisation.

The likes of Johnny Crowley and Séamus Moynihan and a few more, I'd have played against them at schools' level and underage and I'd run through a few things that they might have done previously. All that was essentially left up to me – it wasn't like I was given a dossier or anything like that.

My father was very ill at the time of the Munster final in 1995 – he actually passed away in December of that year. My sister and my mother were very good at insulating me from it but I was definitely quieter than normal that day. I felt very conscious of the event. There was a great picture taken afterwards of me with him and my uncle – Tim Joe – with smiles from ear to ear. My brother, Damien, who lives in the States, posted it on social media again not so long ago. Dad was at that game and he wasn't at too many more after it.

It,s funny when you look back on a game, what is different from what you remember. I looked up the 1995 match on YouTube as part of my research. My first Munster final, a scorching hot day and the place was rocking. I was down at the town side in the first-half; there's a toilet building by the terrace there, and there were people sitting on the roof and there was a garda trying to clear them off. There was a great picture taken of that moment!

The first score was after two minutes and it was a goal for Kerry – Eamonn Breen flicked the ball over my head. Only three minutes earlier, Amhrán na bhFiann was being played and I was looking around, taking it all in and enjoying myself, thinking, *No matter what happens, they can't take this away from me!* Then, ball in the net and you're thinking, *Aw shit, here we go!*

Just before that, I had nearly got cleaned under a high ball but I managed to get it away and about 30 seconds after the goal, I got another ball and I had to kick it with my left leg. My left leg wouldn't have been the greatest at that time, but I got away with it and I did a lot of work on it afterwards. Watching it back, I was thinking I had some first minutes of an introduction!

It mightn't have been a bad thing because I relaxed after that. Tension could have built, waiting for the first goal – the mind could do tricks with you that way – and in a strange way this took a lot of the pressure off me. You're saying to yourself, *That's that over with, anyway!* Now, there could have been another three or four goals and that might have been the end of it, but thankfully that didn't happen.

Maybe I'm looking at it with rose-tinted glasses but there was some fabulous football, and footballers, there that day. Don Davis scored three points; he was awesome that day. It was just a great game. Late on, we were two points up – and this isn't on YouTube, so you'll have to take my word! – there was a chance for Kerry. I think it was just a horrible little toe-poke but there were about 10 people in front of me and it actually managed to come all the way through without a deflection… and it was going in.

Now, I have no doubt I made it look better than it was – but I got absolutely creamed when I got the ball. But making a save like that near the end, I was high as a kite.

In 1998, the management wanted to go in a different direction and Michael Maguire was given the nod as No 1. It was disappointing, but if you're there for 12 years, there's no way you'll be brilliant all the time – there'll be lapses in confidence and form, and you have to roll with the punches. I'd never spit the dummy out and I'd always train hard and whoever else was in there had to train with me. I always knew I'd get a chance and I'd always stick around.

I can remember having a conversation with an inter-county goalkeeper and he was going to pack it in mid-season but I said to him that you either did it at the start of the year or the end of the year. You don't do it during the season, you just keep your mouth shut and your head down – otherwise, you're gone for good. It's just like you see in soccer, a manager comes in and has different ideas: my attitude was to just work harder.

At the end of 1998, to be honest, I didn't know where I stood because the championship ends in mid-summer and everything just comes to a stop. I went away to Australia for five and a half weeks with my buddies at the start of January – and came back in fairly horrific shape! I could have been the number three goalkeeper at the start of that year – there was a couple of other fellas there and I've no doubt I was at the bottom of the pile! But, again, I worked desperately hard to get fit, and I got a chance.

The last match of the regular section of the 1998-99 league was against Dublin in Páirc Uí Rinn, and I was picked. I always loved playing against Dublin as they'd always give you a game of football. I did one or two things I probably wouldn't normally have done, like gone for passes that I wouldn't always have tried… and I got in.

Goalkeeping is like that; you have to take your chance when you get it. You have to grab it. After that, I had done such a body of work to get in shape and I knew that there were others who wouldn't work as hard as me and, maybe it was arrogance again, but the form just lifted.

We ended up playing Dublin again in the league final and I got Man of the Match in that game – I felt I was untouchable at that stage, my head was so far in the clouds. I'd say I was painful to be around, being honest! We all had confidence that year though, it just fed through all of us… I don't know where it came from.

We were on for the double that year. We weren't let up to the hurling final; instead we watched it in the Silver Springs Hotel. I'm not second-guessing management, there's a hard job in getting teams right, but I just think that there were young fellas there that might have benefited from being above for the big day. They were afraid of us being up there and everyone saying, 'It's yer turn now', and I can see their reasoning, but I'd have preferred to have been up there.

Again, like the Munster final in 1995, I loved the occasion. You got the executive train up; it was a treat and I loved every minute of it. Philip Clifford was the captain but he was just a young fella, and I was nearly minding him when Mary McAleese came out. I remember laughing and joking with him in the parade. Fair enough, we lost the game but I really loved that whole experience and I can say that the occasion didn't get to me.

The All-Ireland semi-final against Dublin in 1995 that we lost – that just flew by. Did I do anything wrong? I can't remember anything about it. It was just one of those days that got away from us and I took nothing in. In 1999, I loved it and I thought I performed okay. There were no kickout strategies back then; it was nearly left to your own devices. The first one was short to Ciarán O'Sullivan and the ref decided it was still inside the '21'. I kicked the next one long – to Meath's Johnny McDermott. Some things just looked bigger up there; it seemed like he went 10 feet into the air. After that, I started chipping them to the wings.

Billy used to always say that, as a goalkeeper, you can only mind yourself. What happened out the field was out of your control – though that's probably not the case as much nowadays as they're more involved.

When Páirc Uí Rinn opened in 1993, we played Meath there. If you ever need a trivia question that nobody can answer, ask them who got the first score in a football match at Páirc Uí Rinn – the answer is our full-back Mark O'Connor! I came on for Kerinsie for the last 10 minutes. Meath got a penalty near the end. Brian Stafford took it, and I saved it.

I didn't have a bad record facing them; then again, Colin Corkery was great at rolling the ball to my right in training and always scoring! When I was in Garda College, we had played a Sigerson Cup final in 1995 or '96 against UCD. Trevor Giles took a penalty that day and he rolled the ball to my left.

When Meath got the penalty in the 1999 All-Ireland final, we were two points down and you can see on the video, when it was awarded I was running my hand through my hair, wondering if the game was going away from us. I'll always remember standing there and saying to myself, *This is it, this is what all the hard work was for.*

To be fair, it was a brutally hit penalty but I remembered the one from the Sigerson, dived to my left and saved it. The Cork fans behind me on Hill 16 just went nuts and I had to control myself not to go climbing the fence celebrating, such was the rush of adrenaline!

Human beings are creatures of habit – he was under tremendous pressure as well, as good a player as he was. Would he have remembered the Sigerson?

Maybe, maybe not – he mightn't even have remembered I was in goal – but in an All-Ireland final you'll go for what's most comfortable. It was something I had in the bank from three years earlier and I was going that way.

Cormac Sullivan, the Meath goalkeeper, was very good that year too and I reckon it was the penalty save that sealed the All Star!

We were the form team that year and the regrets are there, definitely. We had 18 wides and we lost by three points. After I saved the penalty, Joe got his goal – we should have driven on after that.

It is a big regret, you can't pretend it's not, but at the end of the day there are fabulous footballers out there – you think of the likes of Declan Browne from Tipp or Kevin O'Brien from Wicklow – that didn't get near an All-Ireland final.

NICHOLAS MURPHY

CORK 0-12 ★ DUBLIN 1-7
NFL Final
Páirc Uí Chaoimh
MAY 9, 1999

★ **CORK:** K O'Dwyer; M O'Donovan, S Óg Ó hAilpín, A Lynch; C O'Sullivan (0-2), O Sexton, M Cronin; Micheál O'Sullivan, **N Murphy**; A Dorgan (0-1), J Kavanagh (0-1), P O'Mahony (0-4); P Clifford (0-4), Mark O'Sullivan, A O'Regan. **Subs:** D Davis for O'Regan, R McCarthy for Murphy.

★ **DUBLIN:** D Byrne; P Moran, P Christie, S Ryan; T Lynch, P Curran, K Galvin; C Whelan (0-1), E Sheehy; J Gavin, D Darcy (0-5), B Stynes; B O'Brien, D Farrell (0-1), N O'Donoghue. **Subs:** D Homan (1-0) for O'Donoghue, J Sherlock for O'Brien.

66

THERE ARE A few games that stand out, including my last-ever inter-county game, when I came on as a sub against Donegal in the 2012 All-Ireland semifinal. Donegal won, obviously, and went on to win the All-Ireland but it was one of the best football matches I've been involved in. Cork could have been a few points ahead in the first-half before Donegal's ferocity got them on top.

The one that sticks out the most though is when I won my first title with Cork, the 1999 league final against Dublin. I had been involved since 1997 – I was an unused sub when Cork lost to Clare above in Ennis – and so getting to a final and winning it was a big thing.

We went on to win the Munster Championship afterwards and obviously lost the All-Ireland final. Winning the league was like a stepping stone.

I don't remember a huge amount about it in terms of detail. I know it was

THE ACTION

★★★★★

CORK WERE FAR superior and, if they were to have had any complaints afterwards, it was that they should have won by more, a 62nd-minute goal from Darren Homan putting an undeserved gloss on the scoreline from Dublin's point of view. Cork dominated midfield, while Joe Kavanagh orchestrated the forward division from No 11 and teenage captain, Philip Clifford gave Shane Ryan plenty of bother in the corner.

By the break, Cork led by 0-5 to 0-3, thanks to some economical play in the forwards, and only for two late frees from Darcy, the lead would have been even more commanding. Cork knew at half-time that their opponents were still in it though, and a good start to the second half would be required if a 10-year wait for a league title would be ended.

They certainly got that good start as the advantage had stretched to six points, 0-10 to 0-4, by the end of the third quarter, with Podsie O'Mahony unlucky not to put the game out of sight when he was denied by a good save from Davy Byrne. Dublin, with a two-man full-forward line of Darcy and Brendan O'Brien, were struggling, and it got even worse for them when sub Jason Sherlock was shown a red card.

The lead had moved to 0-12 to 0-7 by the time of Homan's late intervention, punching home a Dessie Farrell delivery.

★★★★★

on down in Cork, which was unusual for a league final, and Dublin had some hardened players – I was marking Brian Stynes. It was a victory that made it worthwhile, if that makes sense. The two championship games I had been involved in before that were both defeats!

Carrigaline had reached the county intermediate football final in 1996 and I was invited to train with Cork. We lost to Clyda Rovers and I broke my toe, so I couldn't join up with the panel until the start of 1997. I was haunted – I missed all of the infamous running up and down the sand dunes at Inchydoney Beach. The three months of 'Hell' as they were christened… though I did it in subsequent years alright!

I came in, in February – I was still 18 at the time, turning 19 in April. The physicality was the big thing I noticed. I can remember in one of my first sessions, I got an all-merciful belt off Steven O'Brien. I didn't show it, but by God it hurt me! I can remember marking Niall Cahalane and the flaking he gave me. I don't exactly know what Larry Tompkins' thinking was in bringing me in, but either way, it got me used to the whole set-up.

It was definitely a big learning curve for me because I had always been kind of slight growing up, but Tompkins was a big advocate of the gym – it wasn't huge at the start but it definitely crept in over the first couple of years; the gym work was something that we really pushed hard on. It was kind of done wrong in one sense in that it's not like it's done now – we would have done three months of hard gym work and then forget about it for the rest of the year.

As the years passed, we began to do it more in conjunction with our running training and it became a 12-month scenario. I can remember even in 1999, Tompkins had myself and John Miskella, who is the same age as me, doing a load of strength-work because we were younger and he wanted us to get ourselves bigger, because you needed to be at that level. You weren't going to survive if you didn't have some physique.

I was rangy and, because strength and conditioning wasn't big in any team when I was growing up, you didn't have to be as bulky as you would going into an inter-county under-20 team now. Going back 25 years, it wouldn't have been required to have been at the same level. I would have regarded myself as reasonably pacy and because of my long stride I would have been able to get away from tackles.

Midfield was where I always played growing up. In that era, we had huge men around the middle – Pat Hegarty, Liam Honohan, Fachtna Collins. I specifically remember one league match against Armagh in Páirc Uí Rinn. It was a cracking game and I think we beat them by a point, but we started with five midfielders; two conventional ones... and three more in the half-forward line! Obviously, Tompkins' thing was having big guys and physicality. The idea of me playing anywhere else, like full-forward for example, was never seen as an option – basically it was either a natural midfielder or else a wing-forward playing as a third midfielder.

I was in and out of training during the 1996-97 league and it was only after Cork lost the final of that to Kerry that I was brought fully into the squad. I played a few challenge games before the Munster semi-final against Clare. I never thought I'd start but at the same time you're hopeful that you might get a few minutes.

Fachtna and Pat Hegarty started at midfield and they actually had a great game, they got three or four points between them. But all that counted for nothing because Martin Daly scored a last-minute goal to win it for Clare. It was a real 'back down to earth' moment: you're thinking that this isn't going to be plain sailing. The dressing-room afterwards was one of the worst feelings I've ever come across. There was absolutely nothing being said inside there. Everybody was dumbfounded... what could anyone say?

I suppose you have to look back at the amount of hard work the lads had put in. From when Tompkins got them together in October or November, right up to the league final, they were flying fit. Clare were no bad team, but Cork should still have been good enough to get over the line, you would have expected. That was probably the biggest disappointment for the lads – all the work they had put in and the season was over.

Back then, the league used to begin before Christmas and I made my debut against Tipperary in October of 1997. I played a good lot after that. For the championship, Cork were drawn against Kerry in the Munster semi-final in Killarney. I came on for Damien O'Neill to make my championship debut, but Kerry won by a few points. Tompkins was brought back for it – Conor Counihan was part of his management and he was effectively the manager that day, so I

started my championship career with Counihan as my manager and finished with
him as my manager!

By the 1998-99 league, I was established in the team and I do remember one
victory that stood out for us, against Donegal up in Ballybofey. We won by a point. I
think Joe Kavanagh got a goal, and that was a springboard for us. It showed that we
were making progress and really spearheaded the challenge for the eventual league
title. It's never easy to beat Donegal away from home, and we went up there and
won a low-scoring game. It's one I always remember because of how close it was
and how tough it was – I was marking Jim McGuinness that day.

The big thing from when I started, compared to when I finished, was on the
social side of things. Even after that Donegal game, we had a few cans on the way
back – even though Tompkins probably didn't give us the go-ahead – and when
we got back to Cork, we went out for a few drinks because we were on a high. It
was a good buzz and it helped to create a stronger bond.

Even in saying that, it probably wasn't the tightest group I was ever with
– I've never come across one like the team that won the 2010 All-Ireland. In
1999, there were probably groups within the groups, but we all still got on and
did what we had to do. There was a gang of us that started together – myself,
Donagh Wiseman, Anthony Lynch, Seán Óg Ó hAilpín, John Miskella, Alan
Quirke – and we were all fairly close. Then you had another group with Podsie
O'Mahony, Pat Hegarty, Kevin O'Dwyer, for instance. It's not that there was any
friction between the groups, but it just wasn't as tight. In 2010, I'd never have said
it was just me, Graham Canty and the older guys; you could be out with Michael
Shields or Pa Kelly, any age-group and it wouldn't matter. We all just seemed to
be in the same headspace.

We lost two of our seven matches in 1998-99 and we qualified for the knockout
stages; we beat Derry in the quarter-finals and Meath in the semis. Damien
O'Neill, who was a midfielder, had been appointed captain for 1999 when
Bantry Blues won the county championship in '98 but he had to pull out during
the league for work reasons. When that happened, the captaincy would usually
go to a clubmate. Des McAuley, a goalkeeper, had it for a bit in the league, but
then Kevin O'Dwyer won his place back and Philip Clifford was the only other
Bantry starter – he was just 19, but he captained us in the league final. Damien

came back in the early Munster Championship and played against Waterford but then got injured against Limerick and didn't play again after that, so Philip took over again.

Micheál O'Sullivan – Haulie – had come into the team alongside me at midfield during the league and he stayed there. Haulie was a year older than me but we would have grown up playing against each other, and knew a lot about each other and got on well together. The more we played together, the better the partnership became.

Haulie was a much tougher nut than me in terms of physicality, and so we dovetailed – he'd take the more physical guy to allow me to go up and catch the ball. If I knew I couldn't catch it, I'd try to hold back my man to allow him do the fielding. I did think that we worked well together in the sense that both of us knew each other's roles, and respective strengths. It helped the others around us too because everyone knew what our style of play was. It worked well.

The final was a wet day and there wasn't a huge crowd – probably around 10,000 or so. I remember Kevin O'Dwyer having a good game, making a couple of saves, but I still felt that we were in control of the game. We led at half-time but we could have been in front by more. It was physical enough, but we were able to stand up to it and that gave us the belief that we were good enough to win a Munster Championship.

I'd say that there would have been a lot of pressure on Larry, to be fair. In 1998 and '99, he put his faith in a lot of younger fellas – myself, Owen Sexton, Lynchie, Micheál Ó Cróinín, Clifford. There were half a dozen guys there that people didn't know much about. To be fair, they were probably asking why the more seasoned fellas weren't playing with just one or two new fellas brought in, but he took a leap of faith and brought a lot of us on board.

As well as those of us starting, you had Fionán Murray coming off the bench – he had a great goalscoring record that year. In that sense, there was a lot of pressure on Cork going into the league final… and then there was relief that we got over the line.

It was definitely a stepping stone to what we would have hoped would be a fruitful championship campaign – though we know what happened afterwards, it wasn't as fruitful as we would have liked! Winning the league gave us that belief that Cork were a good football team and capable of winning something.

Even now, nearly a quarter of a century on and having won an All-Ireland in 2010, I find it tough to accept losing the '99 final to Meath, and the same with '09 against Kerry. In 2007, Kerry were hands-down the better team, but '99 and '09 always sit badly with me.

I believed that we were good enough to beat Meath. We had beaten them in the league semi-final, even though it was a horrendous game – we won by 0-6 to 0-3! – but it was just one of those games. We had a lot of wides that day. We were unfortunate, too: Steven O'Brien had broken his collarbone in a league match against Galway and that finished him for the year; Colin Corkery was out for whatever reasons; and Aidan Dorgan was injured as well. Michael O'Donovan from Dunmanway was probably the best corner-back in the country that year and he did his collarbone in a challenge match against Sligo.

It's not sour grapes, but it's one of those games that I'd often be thinking as one we could have won and should have won.

MICHEÁL O'SULLIVAN

CORK 2-10 ★ KERRY 2-4
Munster SFC Final
Páirc Uí Chaoimh
JULY 18, 1999

★ **CORK:** K O'Dwyer; R McCarthy, S Óg Ó hAilpín, A Lynch; C O'Sullivan, O Sexton, M Cronin; N Murphy, **Micheál O'Sullivan (0-1)**; B O'Sullivan, J Kavanagh (0-1), P O'Mahony (0-4); P Clifford (0-4), D Davis, Mark O'Sullivan. **Subs:** F Collins (1-0) for B O'Sullivan, F Murray (1-0) for Murphy.

★ **KERRY:** D O'Keeffe; M McCarthy, Barry O'Shea, K Burns; T Ó Sé, S Moynihan, E Breen; D Ó Sé, D Daly; J McGlynn (0-1), L Hassett, D Ó Cinnéide; J Crowley (0-2), A Mac Gearailt (2-0), M Fitzgerald. **Subs:** Billy O'Shea for Hassett, W Kirby (0-1) for McGlynn, MF Russell for Mac Gearailt.

66

WHEN I FIRST started getting interested in Gaelic football at the age of nine or 10, Cork were really starting to pressurise Kerry. Their great team under Mick O'Dwyer was coming to an end and Billy Morgan was building a really strong Cork team. There was always great hype around Munster finals at that time; my father would always have gone along to those games with friends of his, and I started going along with him. It was always the one match you wanted to see... 'When is Cork and Kerry going to be on... and can I go?!'

The grá for playing in a Munster final – and playing against Kerry in a Munster final – would have been building from as far back as then. It was always a dream of mine to take part in such an occasion.

There weren't that many senior teams in West Cork at that time – you had Castlehaven and Clonakilty, and the Carbery divisional team, with Bantry

THE ACTION

★★★★★

AFTER THE LEAGUE win, Cork coasted to Munster Championship victories over Waterford and Limerick to set up a traditional Munster final at home to Kerry.

Injuries to captain Damien O'Neill, Aidan Dorgan, Steven O'Brien and Micheál O'Donovan – outstanding at corner-back during the league – and the unavailability of Colin Corkery might have caused the majority to believe that Kerry would make it four provincial titles on the trot, but the Rebels reigned in the rain, watched by 42,755.

The unusual nature of the day can be summed up by the fact that Maurice Fitzgerald failed to score for Kerry and Páidí Ó Sé's side only scored two points in the second half, one of those by late sub, William Kirby.

Kerry did draw first blood as Aodhán MacGearailt got a goal in the 18th minute, moving them 1-2 to 0-3 in front. Though Philip Clifford levelled for Cork with a pair of points, another Mac Gearailt goal just before half-time sent the Kingdom in with a 2-2 to 0-5 advantage.

Micheál O'Sullivan reduced the arrears to two early in the second period and, with Don Davis covering every blade of glass in a roving rove, Cork pushed on. They were level with 21 minutes to play and then hit the front as sub Fachtna Collins plundered a goal.

The game was made safe as another Cork sub, Fionán Murray, also found the net in the closing stages.

★★★★★

starting to come on the scene. All of the surrounding small clubs used to go to the Castlehaven games back then and fellas my age were dying the see the likes of Larry Tompkins and Niall Cahalane playing big games in real life. It really motivated you to play the game and get involved in the game.

I never played minor for Cork. I went for trials alright in full year minor, 1995, but I ended up getting concussed. I suppose I hadn't been playing that well at the trial anyway but I wasn't invited back! That same year, my club Carbery Rangers from Rosscarbery won the West Cork under-21A championship for the first time and went to a county semi-final. We had a good team and I figured fairly well in that.

After I did the Leaving Cert, I went to college at the University of Limerick and there was a very good group of players a year or two ahead of me, who would have had eyes on winning the Sigerson Cup. I made the Sigerson team when I was in first year and then, by the time I was in second year, 1996-97, I had been called for Cork under-21 trials. I had had a few trials and not been called back; then the Sigerson started and we beat UCC and CIT – Liam Hodnett was a selector with Cork and CIT, and I was brought back on to the under-21 panel. We went all the way to the Sigerson Cup final, but we were beaten by Tralee.

I played two years at under-21, alongside all the guys who made the step up to senior at the same time as myself – Nicholas Murphy, Micheál O'Cróinín, Anthony Lynch, Fionán Murray, Philip Clifford, Brendan Jer O'Sullivan. We probably should have won an under-21 All-Ireland when we had all of those players together, but in 1997 we were beaten by Kerry and then in '98 we were beaten by Declan Browne's Tipperary. Two weeks before we played Tipp in the Munster final, we had played the Cork seniors in a challenge match and we drew with them. I'd say that we thought we were better than what we were and then didn't play as well as we should have in the final, and got caught.

I played a bit of junior with Cork as well over those years and we would have played the seniors in challenge games, so I was starting to get recognised.

I never felt that not playing minor was a handicap. Going to UL was huge, because I was studying PE and we had access to the high-performance gym that Munster Rugby were using. You'd go in there and meet Anthony Foley and Eddie Halvey and John Hayes, and all these fellas. Having access to that and starting to study physical education, taking more of an interest in fitness and taking more time to train all helped. UL would have been training fairly hard for the Sigerson, so that was a big step up in itself – it was probably the next step below senior inter-county.

The lads you were playing with were all of a high standard – of that team that got to the final in 1997, I'd say I was the only fella that hadn't played inter-county. That was a great stepping stone because it really brought you to the level. I was lucky enough to play with the likes of Mike Frank Russell and Dara Ó Cinnéide from Kerry, Jonathan McCarthy from Baile Bhúirne and there were lots of guys from other counties who were already fairly experienced. That all helped in terms of making the step up to senior when the call came.

Ross won the West Cork Junior Championship in 1998. We beat Ilen Rovers and Tadhg Mac Cárthaigh along the way, so I had marked Fachtna Collins and Pat Hegarty – both of whom were on the Cork panel – and I had done fairly well against them. The late Terry O'Neill from Bantry was a selector with Larry at the time and he was never shy about flying the West Cork flag! I was asked in to the panel in late 1998 for the first few National League games before Christmas. The first game I played was against Leitrim in Páirc Uí Rinn, coming on as a sub.

Cork ended up winning the league of 1998-99 and it was huge for confidence. That whole gang of lads that I mentioned, we all came in together and it was all new to us. We had all grown up around the time that Larry was shooting the lights out in the late 1980s and early 1990s, so we'd have run through a wall for him, no questions asked. It was well-documented how hard the team was training and all of us, aged from around 21-23, were able for it. It was three or four nights a week, hard, *hard* stuff, and coming into that league we were in phenomenal shape.

We didn't really fear anyone because we didn't know any better at that age. Then, you had a cohort of really experienced fellas like Don Davis, Ciarán O'Sullivan, Aidan Dorgan and Ronan McCarthy, who had been around for a while and added the other element to it.

Myself and Nicholas came together through good fortune, in a way. Damien O'Neill was the captain but he was out for a while and Liam Honohan was in the mix too, another big player, but he got injured in a league game against Galway. He did come back into the panel after that but struggled to get his place back for the championship. So, you could say that it fell nicely for the two of us, but at the same time we were thrown in at the deep end as two young lads.

It helped that our styles complemented each other. Nick would have been a very good fielder, whereas I wouldn't have been as good at fielding but I was very fit at the time and was covering the ground well. Often during that time, if there was a man-marking job to be done on the opposition's midfield partnership, I'd be taking the man that had to be 'neutralised', shall we say! That then created the option that Nick would be the target for kickouts more often, because he might have an advantage on the other guy. Against Meath, I took John McDermott, and then against Dublin I took Ciarán Whelan and Nick had Brian Stynes.

It did work well – we gelled together in a game-plan where the two of us were operating as sitting midfielders. We were playing a two-man inside line of Mark O'Sullivan and Philip Clifford – Don Davis was named full-forward, but he was coming out the field and then you had the likes of Joe Kavanagh, Podside, Brendan Jer or Micheál Ó Cróinín in the half-forward line, so there was no shortage of talent up front. When the two of us were sitting, it wasn't a blanket defence or anything like that but you automatically had eight men behind the ball if it was turned over.

Damien O'Neill was back for the first two championship games but he was full-forward and Nicholas and myself were given a vote of confidence. We beat Waterford and Limerick well, though unfortunately Damien got injured against Limerick and it was his last match for Cork. They were games we were expected to win and so we were still a bit of an unknown going in against Kerry, but the league run definitely helped. Another help was the fact that the quarter-final against Derry and the semi-final against Meath had been in Croke Park. For a gang of young fellas like us, playing those two games there really benefited us later on in the season.

Then we were lucky that, whatever way the arrangement between Cork and Dublin fell, the league final against them was in Páirc Uí Chaoimh that year. Dublin were no bad team either – they had won the All-Ireland only four years previously – but, in fairness, we performed very well on the day.

I had been going well in the league and I played reasonably well against Waterford. Against Limerick, I was taken off – I had been marking John Quane, a big, strong midfielder, and to be fair to him, he was one of the toughest fellas I ever came across. I just ran out of gas and ran out of power with about 15 minutes to go and I was replaced, so that did an element of doubt there as regards whether I was any way sure of my position for the Munster final or not. Thankfully, I was picked alongside Nicholas.

At the time, we were a very motivated team and, having won the league and the McGrath Cup before it, we were expecting to go places. We had got into a Munster final and we were on a roll. It was a very settled team, and Tompkins had us flying fit and well-motivated. There wasn't any fear there going into the game, really. Kerry were probably the favourites but we knew that we were in a great position to take them on.

Earlier on in the year, we had played Kerry – I think it was the opening of Mayfield's new pitch. I was marking Darragh Ó Sé that day and did reasonably well on him. It was the same when we played them in the league below in Killarney, so I was lucky enough to have two cuts off him before we met in the Munster final in Páirc Uí Chaoimh. Their other midfielder was Donal Daly, and Nick would have had an aerial advantage over him to give us an outlet for our kickouts. There's no doubt that Darragh was the best midfielder I've ever marked because he was a great fielder and a great footballer. He had the aggression and he had the mentality.

That day, things worked out for us. We had a thing going where we'd try to go around him – Kevin O'Dwyer our goalkeeper and the two wing-backs Ciarán O'Sullivan and Martin Cronin and myself. We were trying to open up a space outside the wing-back, and Kevin would kick it over the lads' heads and I'd try to run on to it rather than hanging in the air with Darragh. He was a renowned fielder and we all knew that but we were trying to take his strengths away from him!

It was a rotten day, but the weather didn't really have an effect; at the end of the day, it was the same for both teams. Aodhán Mac Gearailt got two great goals for Kerry in the first-half – funnily enough, we would end up teaching together in Carrigaline for a few years! – but we stayed with them and gradually got on top. Aodhán was actually taken off in the second-half by Páidí Ó Sé and he wasn't too impressed.

Fachtna Collins and Fionán Murray came on and both of them scored goals, and they helped to put us five or six points up. It was a full house and the Cork crowd were driving us on. Once we got back in front with those goals, it was going to be our day. It was my first Munster final at senior level and it was a huge personal achievement to have made a team and to be playing Kerry on such a stage. It was all about trying to perform then on the day and get the best out of yourself. I was lucky enough that it went very well for me and I got Man of the Match.

Confidence grew from there and we beat Mayo in the All-Ireland semi-final, and then just fell short against Meath in the final. We kicked something like 19 wides that day against Meath in the final. Even if we'd got half of them, we would have won the game handily.

We definitely could or should have won that All-Ireland but, as a group of young fellas, we thought we'd be back there every second year. It hurt, but we expected that there'd be another chance. It took an awful long time for Cork to come back, as we saw.

Thankfully, that disappointment doesn't affect my memories of the Munster final. It was a day that went well for me and it's always something I'll be able to look back on.

99

25

OF THE
GREATEST
IN ACTION

★★★★★

★

*Beating Kerry in 1996 was
the 'Game of his Life' for Con
Paddy O'Sullivan*

★

*Billy Morgan (below) shakes hands
with Liam Sammon of Galway before
the 1973 All-Ireland final*

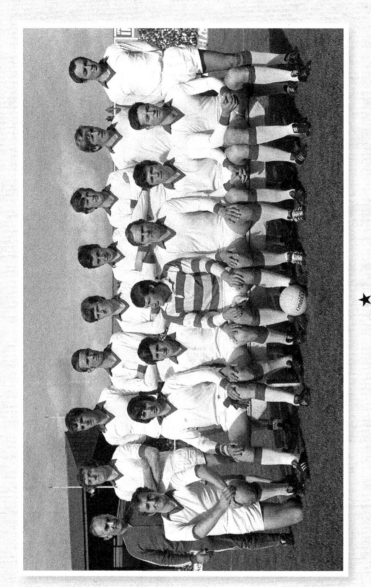

John Coleman and the Cork team which defeated Galway in the 1973 All-Ireland final

Tadhg Murphy, second from right behind No. 7 Jimmy Kerrigan, celebrates after scoring Cork's last minute winning goal against Kerry in the 1983 Munster final

John Cleary (left) races through the Mayo defence in the 1989 All-Ireland final

Conor Counihan and the Cork team that defeated Mayo in the 1989 All-Ireland final

Colman Corrigan during
Cork's breakthrough
Munster final victory over
Kerry in 1987

★
Paul McGrath rounds
Meath's Martin
O'Connell in the 1988
All-Ireland final replay

Tony Davis chases down Liam McHale of Mayo in the 1989 All-Ireland final

★
*Dinny Allen lifts Sam
high after Cork defeated
Mayo in 1989*

★
*Larry Tompkins
leads the Cork
team out onto
the field before
the 1990 All-
Ireland final*

★
Niall Cahalane has Colm O'Rourke all wrapped up in the 1990 All-Ireland final

★
Joe Kavanagh in action against Mayo in the 1999 All-Ireland semi-final

★
Ciarán O'Sullivan beats Dara O'Cinneide to the ball in Cork's last great victory over Kerry in Killarney

★

Kevin O'Dwyer acknowledges supporters during the pre-match parade ahead of the 1999 All-Ireland final against Meath

Nicholas Murphy competes high with Meath's John McDermott in the 1999 All-Ireland final

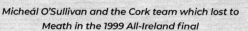

Micheál O'Sullivan and the Cork team which lost to Meath in the 1999 All-Ireland final

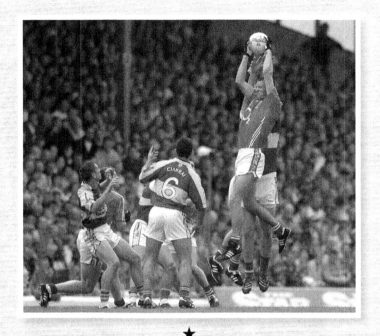

Pearse O'Neill rises highest to claim the ball against Kerry in the Munster final in the summer of 2007

Patrick Kelly breaks away from Owen Mulligan of Tyrone in Cork's epic win in the 2009 All-Ireland semi-final against the reigning champs

Derek Kavanagh celebrates the final whistle after the 2010 All-Ireland final against Down

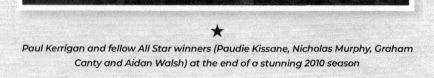

★
Paul Kerrigan and fellow All Star winners (Paudie Kissane, Nicholas Murphy, Graham Canty and Aidan Walsh) at the end of a stunning 2010 season

★

Graham Canty lifts the Sam Maguire Cup high after victory over Down in 2010

*Daniel Goulding celebrates after hitting Cork's ninth point in
the All-Ireland victory over Down in 2010*

★
Mark Collins and Seán Powter celebrate Cork's late victory over Kerry in 2020

★
Ian Maguire races through the Mayo defence during the 2023 All-Ireland Championship

PEARSE O'NEILL

KERRY 0-10 ★ CORK 0-10
Munster SFC Final
Fitzgerald Stadium
JULY 9, 2006

★ **KERRY:** D Murphy; A O'Mahony, M McCarthy, M Ó Sé; T Ó Sé, S Moynihan, M Lyons; D Ó Sé, K Donaghy; P Galvin, E Brosnan, B Sheehan; C Cooper, D O'Sullivan, P O'Connor. **Subs:** T O'Sullivan for Lyons, D O'Sullivan for O'Connor, T Griffin for T Ó Sé.

★ **CORK:** A Quirke; M Prout, K O'Connor (0-1), G Canty; M Shields, G Spillane, A Lynch; D Kavanagh, **P O'Neill**; S O'Brien, N Murphy, K MacMahon (0-1); J Masters (0-7), F Goold (0-1), D O'Connor. **Subs:** O Sexton for O'Connor, K O'Sullivan for O'Brien, C McCarthy for O'Neill, D Niblock for Goold.

66

WAS THIS THE best game I played for Cork? No. What it was about was how I arrived into the team. For instance, three weeks before the Munster final that year, I wasn't even on the Cork panel!

What happened was that, in around November 2005, myself and two lads from home – Ger Melvin and Paul Kilbane – struck off for Australia. I was just about to turn 26. We were going to stay for the year, but in around March or April I began to get homesick, as simple as that. I said I'd head back home, and the two lads stayed on.

I arrived home about a week or so before we played Na Piarsaigh in the first round of the county senior championship in April 2006. We beat them inside in Ballinacurra by a point, a very tight and close game, typical first-round encounter.

The win put us into the fourth round and in the middle of June, we played

THE ACTION

★★★★★

CORK'S LAST WIN over Kerry had been in the 2002 Munster semi-final, while there had been four defeats since then – the advent of the back door and a second chance had resulted in All-Ireland semi-final defeats to the Kingdom in Croke Park in 2002 and '05.

The 2006 campaign would end in the same fashion but this result marked an improvement for Cork and they would go on to triumph in the replay, albeit suffering the loss of key defender Graham Canty to a cruciate ligament injury.

Billy Morgan's side started like a train, their appetite for the battle displayed in the turnover that led to Kevin MacMahon's opening point. When Kieran O'Connor – superb throughout in defence, as was Ger Spillane – sent over a point around the 25-minute mark, the visitors led by 0-7 to 0-1.

Unfortunately for Cork, a questionable red card for Anthony Lynch allowed Kerry to claw their way back into the contest and by half-time the score was 0-7 to 0-4. When Bryan Sheehan sent over a point near the end, Kerry had the lead for the first time but Cork responded. After a good Nicholas Murphy win in the air, Kevin MacMahon was fouled and James Masters levelled.

Despite being the team to equalise, Cork felt regret at not winning, given such a strong start. Still, they had avoided defeat and had a second chance, at home the following Sunday. The final word went to Cork selector John Corcoran.

★★★★★

Naomh Abán in Páirc Uí Rinn. We used to play them quite a lot around that time and we always had good battles with them, but we beat them by a few points, 1-10 to 0-8.

Around the same time, Cork played Limerick in the Munster football semi-final – it was a poor game and they only won by a few points. Dermot Hurley from Castlehaven was on the panel and he broke a bone in his wrist, so they were down a midfielder. I got a call on a Monday, just under three weeks out from the final, from Ger O'Sullivan from Dromtarriffe, who was a selector with Billy Morgan. He said they were doing something that night and asked if I'd come on away up?

I said I'd give it a go and around three days later we played Clare in a challenge match in Ennis. I started the game and I did okay; then about a week later we played Westmeath, and I started that too and did okay. Then, I was named in the team for the Munster final!

It was going to be my first time getting on the pitch in a Cork jersey. I had never played minor but I was on the under-21 panel in 2000 – Cork lost to a good Limerick team that had John Galvin and Stephen Lucey on it, but I didn't get any game-time.

One thing about this all happening so quickly was that I didn't have any time to think about whether I was ready or able for it. I was playing away hurling and football for Aghada and then, before I knew it, I was going to be starting a Munster final for Cork. I just kind of went with it.

I wouldn't have known too many guys on the panel. Maybe a few from when I was on the under-21 squad but that was a fairly short year. You'd know players from going up against them in the club championship and stuff, but I wouldn't have been hugely familiar with a lot of them. I would have played in a couple of trial matches a few years previously, so I would have known Billy a little bit but, again, not a lot.

I went into the two challenge games with the attitude, *I've nothing to lose here. If I don't play well or whatever, that's fine… but if I do play well, it's a big opportunity.* A few things fell into place at the right time, but it could easily have gone another way.

After both of the challenge matches, I can remember talking to Billy and he was saying that I was going well. He'd be a very good man-manager and the message was to keep motoring. It was good feedback to get but, obviously, I didn't know if I'd be starting or anything. It was all moving so quickly, but around a week out from the Kerry game it dawned on me that I could be starting. Then the team was named on the Tuesday night and I was selected at centre-forward, one of seven Munster final debutants along with Alan Quirke, Michael Prout, my fellow Aghada man Kieran O'Connor, Michael Shields, Ger Spillane and Donncha O'Connor.

After I went to Australia, my gang at home actually booked a trip out to visit me during the summer. It would have been too much hassle to cancel the trip when I came home, so, when I was making my Cork debut, they were all out in Oz watching me! There would always be some few around the home house and there's a big lot of us, but I was there on my own preparing for the game, which was very unusual.

We never won in Killarney during my time with Cork but this game was the first of three straight draws there – 2006, '08 and '09. I always loved playing there. We used to go to the Castlerosse Hotel, land down at around half past 10 or 11 and have a bite to eat and walk around outside. The crowds would be building and you'd have the team-talk down there, before getting on the bus and heading to the stadium. That bus journey from the hotel to the pitch used to be unreal, a great buzz.

I was trying to tell myself to keep things simple. Obviously, I had no experience of any of this so I knew there was no point in trying anything too fancy. It was just about doing the basic things right, getting the ball and moving it on quickly because I knew the pace was going to be very quick. You're trying to feel your way into the game and get a bit more comfortable.

I ended up playing a good bit of the game at midfield, up against Kieran Donaghy – a year and a half earlier, we had been playing together for *The Underdogs* on the TV show! I would have known him quite well, so it was weird to be marking him in a Munster final, all of a sudden.

The thing about *The Underdogs* in 2004 was that I didn't even go for the initial trials or anything. I was just playing away with the club and then someone got on to me in the late summer that year to say that they were short a midfielder or two, and would I think about going for it. They were playing Limerick and I turned up – I was named midfield with Donaghy that night and it went well enough. That was late enough in the whole process but – like with Cork in 2006 – without over-thinking it, I said I'd go for it.

I remember after about two or three minutes, there was a kickout and I went up for it, with Donaghy coming from behind me. There's a picture of it in some pub in Tralee, I think – one of the lads sent it to me one day – and it shows Donaghy basically using my shoulders as a ladder, a mile off the ground and fetching the ball. That was after only a couple of minutes and I was thinking, *This is going to be a long day here!* After that, I worked my into it and the game itself was typical Cork and Kerry.

We had a great start, up 0-7 to 0-1 in the first-half, but had a player sent off before half-time. Kerry came back in the second-half, though they went down to 14 midway through, and the game played its way out. If I remember rightly, we could have had a free towards the end; James Masters was half-fouled, but we didn't get it and it was a draw. Nearly every game we played down there was tit-for-tat and tight towards the end.

The feeling was that we had had a good rattle off them, so there was no reason we couldn't do it back in Páirc Uí Chaoimh, and that's what happened in the replay. It took a few more years to go from that to an All-Ireland but it was a great journey.

I was lucky enough to be there for eight years or so, playing under two brilliant managers in Billy and Conor Counihan, who I obviously would have known from Aghada, and great management teams. There was a great bond among the players – it's easy to say that and nearly every team would claim to have it – but we actually did. We always got on well and there was never any under-current or anything in the panel. It was always very united and honest. Everyone was up front with each other.

Could we have won more? Of course we could but, looking back now, I didn't play with Cork until I was 26 and I won and All-Ireland and four Munsters, and met some great lads along the way. It was a very fond time.

99

PATRICK KELLY

CORK 1-13 ★ TYRONE 0-11
All-Ireland SFC semi-final
Croke Park
AUGUST 23, 2009

★ **CORK:** A Quirke; R Carey, M Shields, A Lynch; N O'Leary, G Canty, J Miskella; A O'Connor (0-1), N Murphy; P Kerrigan (0-1), P O'Neill (0-1), **P Kelly (0-2)**; D Goulding (1-1), C O'Neill (0-2), D O'Connor (0-4). **Subs:** F Goold (0-1) for Goulding, J Hayes for Kerrigan, M Cussen for O'Connor, K O'Connor for O'Leary, E Cadogan for Miskella.

★ **TYRONE:** P McConnell; PJ Quinn, C Gormley, R McMenamin (0-1); D Harte (0-1), Justin McMahon, P Jordan (0-1); K Hughes (0-1), E McGinley; B Dooher, T McGuigan, Joe McMahon; M Penrose (0-1), Stephen O'Neill (0-4), O Mulligan (0-2). **Subs:** B McGuigan for T McGuigan, S Cavanagh for McGinley, Seán O'Neill for Gormley, A Cassidy for Dooher, C McCullagh for Joe McMahon.

66

THIS WAS ONE of those frantic games, really high-energy. Thinking back now, it's amazing how different it was – the game changed so much in such a short space of time. It was still very traditional, man for man, a lot of ball kicked into the full-forward line for 50-50 battles. Kickout strategies were non-existent… basically, it was a case of just launching it. There were loads of turnovers and none of the long passages of play where one team keeps possession for a few minutes.

It felt like one of the biggest wins that group ever had, beating the All-Ireland champions. Getting the good start was crucial – Colm O'Neill kicked a few big scores, and Pearse O'Neill and Paul Kerrigan got some, too. A lot of the forwards got on the ball early and it was one of those where we got ahead and that cushion was huge then after we went down to 14. I don't think they ever even got it back to three points.

THE ACTION

★★★★★

AFTER A NARROW All-Ireland semi-final replay loss to Kerry in 2008, Conor Counihan's first full season in charge had seen Cork waltz to a Division 2 league title before seeing off Kerry on the way to a Munster final win over Limerick.

In the All-Ireland quarter-final against Donegal, Cork were regal in a 1-27 to 2-10 win but there was little doubt that a stiffer challenge was in store against All-Ireland champions Tyrone. By the end of the first quarter of an hour, all of the Cork starting forwards had scored and, between the eighth and 15th minutes, Cork outscored their opponents 1-5 to no score, Daniel Goulding with the goal.

By half-time, the Red Hands had reduced the gap slightly, to 1-9 to 0-7, but they also now had the advantage of possessing an extra man after O'Connor's red card for a second bookable offence. Many in Croke Park must have anticipated that Cork would be hanging on after the restart, but the reality was nothing of the sort. Solid defending prevented Tyrone from every harnessing any kind of momentum and the shuttling back of wing-forwards Patrick Kelly and Paul Kerrigan ensured that the numerical disadvantage never felt like a factor.

When sub Fintan Goold rounded off a good move to leave Cork 1-13 to 0-11 in front, the Rebel faithful could breathe easy and marvel at a job well done.

★★★★★

My age-group in Ballincollig was pretty decent, but I never felt like a stand-out player. We had five Cork minors in 2003 – Colin Weste was the main man and he got most of the limelight in the club. We got to under-16 and minor county finals, and we were always playing at the top grade. Coláiste Choilm were always playing at a high level in colleges' GAA too in terms of the Corn Uí Mhuirí but I certainly don't think I'd have been ear-marked for greater things. I played a Cork under-16 trial out in Ovens and I only touched the ball once or twice. I was probably too nervous.

I played minor for Cork in 2003, and under-21 in 2004, '05 and '06. We won three Munster under-21 titles and lost an All-Ireland final to Mayo – the lads beat Laois then the next year.

Around Christmas before my last year of under-21, I was called for senior trials and the same the following year. At the time, the Duhallow under-21 competition was running and I was playing in that for Ballincollig – two years in-a-row, I got injured playing in that, the night before Cork trials. I didn't go for them and I didn't get them. In any case, I don't think I'd have been anywhere near the standard going into my last year under-21 – the following year I might have, but I wouldn't have expected it.

From my group, Alan O'Connor and John Hayes were the only ones who made it quite young. The year after us had a glut of lads – Paul Kerrigan, Daniel Goulding, Fintan Goold, Ray Carey, Eoin Cadogan, Michael Shields. My first year out of under-21, 2007, when Cork got to the All-Ireland final and lost to Kerry, was my first time in four years not being involved with Cork, but I wouldn't have said I was knocking at the door or anything.

After Billy Morgan left following the 2007 season and Teddy Holland's appointment, there was a strike and then Conor Counihan took over. That meant a late start in 2008 and there was a trawl for players. I had started in Mary I, and I got a call from John Miskella saying that there was a trial match and Conor wanted me to attend. It was an intra-squad match on a Friday night and then I got asked to go to Wexford on the Sunday for a challenge game, and it just went from there.

After the 2007 season, I felt that I was young enough that I'd be called for trials again. I was out of UCC so I was copping on a small bit – I probably wasn't the most dedicated when I was there – and I trained savage hard to be ready in case a call came and to give it more commitment than I had.

I would have played with Goulding a lot in Coláiste Choilm, Niall Horgan from Glen Rovers and St Nicholas (and now the owner of Gym + Coffee) was there too – he was dual Cork minor captain in 2003. I did definitely take it seriously and I was trying to focus on football at 17, but I didn't feel like I was destined to play for Cork or anything. I was as into soccer as I was GAA when I was growing up. I packed in the hurling with Ballincollig after under-16 as I wanted to make the Cork minor football panel… and I was useless at hurling anyway!

I always played midfield growing up, even up to my first few years at senior level with the club. I was never a fielder, obviously – at minor level I played alongside Alan O'Connor and let him do the catching! It was the same with Michael Cussen for UCC Freshers and in the Sigerson Cup. I was always a fella who went the other side or went for the breaks.

For the school, I often played in the forwards and the same if I was playing up an age. My first year under-21, I played centre-forward so it wasn't totally alien when I was put in the half-forward line for Cork seniors. With the midfielders that were available, it was clear that was the only place I was going to get in. With that role, I wasn't particularly fast or strong or a huge scorer, so I had to be a worker. Brian Dooher was in his pomp then for Tyrone, the same with Paul Galvin for Kerry – what they were doing was what I was trying to do.

Tactics back then were worlds apart from what they are now. It was still fairly basic. Tyrone obviously had brought some intensity around the middle, with having more bodies there, but it still hadn't gone to the blanket defences or anything. You had maybe one wing-forward who worked back – I was one wing and Kerrigan was on the other, so it was natural that it was me who was going back more often than him. I didn't think that centre-forward was an option. Pease was there and at the time centre-backs were stoppers, so the wings were a better place to hide!

When I came in first, I would have said that I was doing well to be on the squad. I wasn't exactly out of my depth but I definitely felt that I wasn't ready. The physicality in training was an eye-opener and I wouldn't have been as fit as other lads. After the end of 2008, I made a big effort over that winter, knowing that I'd get a shot in the McGrath Cup and maybe the league. I got lucky – I got in and it stuck.

I made my championship debut in the 2008 Munster semi-final up in Limerick. That year, myself and Kerrigan were subs – I came on against Limerick, he came on in the Munster final… then I came on again against Kildare in the All-Ireland quarter-final. Cork had been ahead by a good bit and then Kildare came back; about the only thing I did was make a block towards the end. We played Kerry in the All-Ireland semi-final and came back from seven points down to draw, before they won the replay – I didn't get a run in either of those two games, and Kerrigan came on in the second one.

Back then, there was Kevin MacMahon, Conor McCarthy, Seán O'Brien, Fintan Goold all fighting for places on the wings and they were all unbelievably fit fellas who definitely had it over me there. I wasn't sitting on the bench thinking that I should have been starting but, the next year, once I was at their level in terms of fitness, I would have felt that I had enough football to have a chance of getting in. I was lucky that things fell into place.

I would have been physically weak and, prior to coming in in 2008, I wouldn't have done weights at all. With Cork under-21s, we were given gym membership and programmes and I'd say I went once, maybe. As soon as I went in with the seniors, I was lucky that Goulding was living close by and we used to go to the gym together. He was very dedicated, so through 2008 and that winter, it kind of became an obsession to make it. I realised that if you don't make it in the first couple of years, you're not going to make it. I definitely would have been very single-minded in terms of trying to improve, because I knew that my chance was going to come early in 2009. We won the McGrath Cup, so I got a few games there and being in the team from the start of the league helped me in keeping the place.

Being honest, watching the Kerry games in the 2008 All-Ireland semi-final, I would have thought that they were the better team and a bit ahead of us, as good as the comebacks by Cork were in both matches. Come 2009, the players from the 2007 under-21 team were a couple of years out of that grade and more established at senior.

You had a very mature group – the older lads obviously, but the guys coming through were very mature too – and it was going to be the team's first full year with Conor. Peadar Healy was a very good coach and Aidan O'Connell was an excellent strength and conditioning guy – fellas were saying it was a big improvement on anything they'd ever had before.

There wasn't any real need for hand-holding; I think fellas were very, very dedicated and it gelled nicely. The league success sparked a bit of confidence, even if it was only Division 2, and the influx of seven or eight players over a couple of years, nearly all starters, pushed the group on a bit.

We drew in Killarney in 2009, after playing well. It was definitely seen as an opportunity lost and it's probably one we'd still have regrets about, especially given that Cork still haven't won there since 1995. At the same time, any time we brought Kerry back to Cork, we were more confident; I'm not sure if it's a psychological thing or what. That game was quite a comfortable one, we won fairly well even if it wasn't a hammering.

The comeback to beat Kerry in 2008 in the rain was great, but this was a more solid victory. There would have been a belief that we were getting very close – Kerry and Tyrone were the big two obviously, but Cork had been to the final in 2007 and semi-finals in 2008 and so were the next best.

That win gave those of us starting for the first time a big belief that we were good enough and that the team was good enough. Goulding had begun establishing himself more and myself and Kerrigan got in on the wings, and Colm O'Neill came later in the summer. There was an evolution in the forward line and maybe it gave a bit more energy to us.

After beating Kerry, we had Limerick at home in the Munster final and it needed a bit of a comeback in the second-half to make sure of the win. You look at Cork losing to Tipp in the Munster final in 2020, after beating Kerry – it's that whole idea of getting yourself back up mentally for a game that, on paper, people expect you to win.

To be fair, Limerick were very good at that time and they were very competitive. They were very unlucky not to turn us or Kerry over. I had played with Ian Ryan in Mary I and he had just come on the scene; he scored a good bit that day. They had John Galvin in midfield and Seánie Buckley up front. They had Johnny McCarthy, Stephen Lucey and Stephen Lavin in the back – they were a physical team and whenever we played them it was never a hammering. They were able to stop our running game and we never put them to the sword. Even in 2010, in the qualifiers up in Limerick, they took us to extra time. We never took them for granted, either.

That day in 2009, it was about just getting over the line and it was a great way to be coming out of Munster, because there was no cockiness or arrogance. If there were any egos after Kerry, they were well back down before leaving Munster, thanks to Limerick.

We had Donegal in the All-Ireland quarter-final. It was my first big game starting in Croke Park – the same for Colm and Paul – and that definitely brings a different kind of pressure, especially with the travelling and the hype around the game. Donegal were decent back then, but I don't think that they were considered genuine All-Ireland contenders.

We were expected to win and we blitzed them early; I think we were up by 10 points at half-time. It was very one-sided and they didn't play well at all. In comparison to the fitness and the physicality that we had, I thought that they were way off it. And then within two years they had won Ulster, before winning the All-Ireland the following year!

For the newer guys, that game was massive leading in to the Tyrone match as it gave us all a dry run for a bigger and more nerve-wracking game. It was a handy one but at the same time they're good to get under your belt, as you get used to the rhythms of the weekend. The travel, the hotel you stay at, the pre-match meal, everything... for a young and inexperienced player, it was ideal.

For a Sunday game, we'd always go up on the Saturday – it varied between bus and train. For Conor's first year and a bit, we used to stay at the Burlington and then we started going out to Killiney because, for the big games, having a bit of a crowd around is a nuisance. We were lucky that we were up in Dublin a good bit for league finals and championship games, so that familiarity and routine became comforting. The pre-match nerves wouldn't exactly disappear but there was a calm within the group, having all those little things, like table-tennis tables, PlayStations and so on. All of that helped to build the squad and the camaraderie.

The older guys like Alan Quirke, Anthony Lynch, Nicholas Murphy, Graham Canty, John Miskella would have gone through a lot, with bad defeats in the early 2000s to Limerick, Roscommon and Fermanagh, so they were very tight already, but those weekends away helped everyone to bond. The younger crew got on very well with the older crew from early on.

When you're winning and you're coming home from these matches, it just all adds to the team spirit. They were happy days.

Conor was a tough manager, probably like Billy was before him. He didn't suffer fools. He was simple in that there were no fancy speeches or anything like that, but the group was very driven. The older lads led it by example – the likes of Derek Kavanagh and Seán O'Brien were ferocious trainers, even though they mightn't have been starters by that time. There was a great sense of satisfaction when we played A-versus-B games and there was no weak link. You were dreading having to go and mark any fella on the B team – that's often an overstated cliché, but there was a serious squad there and things just clicked.

The older fellas were very hungry. They had suffered the 2007 defeat to Kerry, and lost semi-finals to them and they really drove it. They preferred how things were by this time, in terms of diet and preparation and analysis and all of that. For the younger fellas, we were just lapping up what they were telling us. It was a nice group that came together – it doesn't always work that way, as we found out a few years later. Things can go wrong very quickly if the mixture isn't right.

It was the first summer I found that I was being asked a lot of questions about matches. You'd meet someone in the shop and they'd ask, 'How are you fixed for Sunday?' Or whatever else. Previously, when I was just a sub, that wasn't happening as much, so the amount of interaction was noticeable.

Kevin Clancy was brought in as sports psychologist and I remember, a few weeks before the Tyrone game, he gave us all scripts in terms of how to respond to questions from journalists or anyone else. It wasn't quite to fob people off, more to get your head thinking right. Someone would ask how we were fixed and the answer was, 'Tyrone are a great team; we're going to have to be at our best to beat them'. There were two or three pointers but the main thing was that if we performed, we'd give them a good game. You were encouraged to repeat these few lines to avoid getting into nitty-gritty conversations.

It was the first time I used anything like that. In 2008, when I was a sub, I'd chat away because I didn't have the same nerves. In 2009, that was very handy because you'd be popping down to club training or matches and, naturally, the conversation would go towards the big match. The last thing you wanted was to get into an in-depth conversation about injuries or the team or whatnot.

You always knew when you were playing a championship match as your body would be giving you the signs. I'd get nervous, like everyone else, but never recklessly nervous. I was never one for superstitions, though – I always made a point of avoiding rituals around buses or who I sat with, as I don't believe in them.

We had been up in Croke Park three times in 2008, and then in '09 there was the league final and the Donegal match, so I had been lucky enough to be up there a good few times before the Tyrone game. I know it's a cliché but you're just going through the process in terms of your prep and your mindset. Clancy would have been big on visualisation; how you just walk through your day in advance. One of the selectors, Jim Nolan, would have all the logistics arranged in terms of times, and you'd have to wear certain gear on the Saturday and then different gear on the Sunday. You'd have been told what time the bus would leave, how long the warm-up would be, what time you go on the pitch, whether there's a parade or an anthem… all those things, and Clancy would have made sure that we had gone through it all. You weren't dreaming about the hat-trick or the winning point, just familiarising yourself with the day as a whole.

On top of that, goal-setting became a big thing. As a wing-forward, what were the two or three big things you were going to focus on to get on breaking ball or opportunities to get a score or break tackles. Those small things I devoured. At underage, I would have played a lot more off the cuff, whereas I found that this took away the nerves a bit. You were focusing on a couple of controllables in terms of what you could do, so I felt that the group were getting all the right kind of modern thinking and coaching. All of those steps helped us along the way.

Cork had never beaten Kerry in Croke Park, and Kerry hadn't beaten Tyrone there in the 2000s. Rather than there being a fear factor around playing them, what was there was an energy that it was a big opportunity. That group had been unlucky to meet Kerry nearly every time in Croke Park, rather than Dublin, Armagh, Mayo or Tyrone, so we felt that this was a good chance to test ourselves against a big gun and beat them.

This was a fresh team – as well as the few of us coming into the attack, Ray Carey and Shieldsy had established themselves in defence, and Alan O'Connor was making a midfield spot his own. It wasn't exactly a free hit, but it was game with no baggage. There was no talk of a psychological barrier or anything. Tyrone were obviously All-Ireland champions but that meant that they were a scalp to be taken and if we could do that, it would show that we were in the top bracket of teams.

I can't remember how it happened but I ended up playing right half-forward, being marked by Philip Jordan, with Kerrigan on the left and Davy Harte on him. Again, for someone like me just in, being marked by someone with three All-Irelands felt daunting. My thing basically was just to keep running – a very simple gameplan.

We got a decent start, even though we missed a couple of chances very early on. The goal came when Canty broke forward; Colm had a shot blocked and Goulding roofed it. I got a point straight after that, from the kickout, and then we went four, five… six ahead. We might have even stretched it to eight – we were well up, though they still had a couple of goal chances. Alan was sent off with five or 10 minutes to go before half-time and they were down to four by the break.

From memory, Pearse went back from centre-forward to midfield alongside Aidan Walsh. Donncha O'Connor came to the half-forward line and we left Colm and Daniel inside. It was kind of ready-made in that there was no need for a change in personnel. I think we only got four points in the second-half, but the intensity and the workrate were huge. Tyrone weren't at their best either and Seán Cavanagh, who had been Footballer of the Year in 2008, wasn't able to start – though I think I didn't realise he wasn't playing until he came on as a sub! That sounds bizarre but it shows the bubble we were in.

It was definitely one of the sweetest wins we had, if not the sweetest, in terms of a performance independent of any other context. Obviously, there's the after-taste of what followed against Kerry in the All-Ireland final and that will always put it down the pecking order a little bit, but I do think that this win did help for the following year, and there were important foundations like that. For example, when people look back at the 2010 All-Ireland, the win over Dublin in the semi-final is as significant as the final in the way we won it.

Dublin in 2010 was a full house, with massive pressure – having that experience of going into a huge game really helped. There was a crowd of around 55,000 for the Tyrone match; it wasn't the same cauldron but it was still a huge game. Quarter-finals aren't the same – a double-header and Cork wouldn't be bringing a huge crowd so it doesn't have the same feeling, especially as they were games you were expected to win.

I do think that this was a game that gave us belief that that squad was good enough. Obviously, losing the final to Kerry was horrendous but we did come back after 2009 with a real belief that there was an All-Ireland within touching distance. It was just a case of getting that bit better again. It was felt that that Kerry team was maybe a couple of years ahead of us and they were reaching or passing their peak, whereas our trajectory was upwards.

We won the league in 2010 to back that up, so you're coming off winning Division 2 and then Division 1, coupled with beating Tyrone in an All-Ireland semi-final – there's massive confidence that you're right there. I don't think you could over-state how important or satisfying the Tyrone game was from that point of view.

99

DEREK KAVANAGH
(& PAUL KERRIGAN)

CORK 1-15 ★ DUBLIN 1-14
All-Ireland SFC Semi-Final
Croke Park
AUGUST 22, 2010

★ **CORK:** A Quirke; R Carey, M Shields, J Miskella; N O'Leary, G Canty, P Kissane; A O'Connor, A Walsh (0-1); **P Kerrigan (0-1)**, P O'Neill, P Kelly (0-2); D Goulding (0-4), C Sheehan, D O'Connor (1-5). **Subs:** E Cadogan for Canty, N Murphy for A O'Connor, C O'Neill (0-1) for Sheehan, **D Kavanagh (0-1)** for Miskella, F Goold for O'Leary.

★ **DUBLIN:** S Cluxton; M Fitzsimons, R O'Carroll, P McMahon (0-1); K Nolan, G Brennan, C O'Sullivan; R McConnell (0-1), MD McAuley (0-1); N Corkery, A Brogan (0-2), B Cullen (0-1); D Henry, E O'Gara, B Brogan (1-7). **Subs:** B Cahill for O'Sullivan, P Flynn for Henry, E Fennell for Corkery, C Keaney (0-1) for O'Gara, D Bastick for O'Carroll.

"

OUR MAIN LEARNING from 2007, '08 and '09 was the need for a streak of ruthlessness and it was hard learned.

It was beginning to show in 2009 and in '10 that we were just a bit more street-wise and game-wise. In 2007, we didn't have the street-smarts but after that, we became very angry as a group. We knew that we were good footballers but as individuals we were nice guys and that maybe translated to playing the game by the rules and with the best sentiment. We learned that you have to be a bit more ruthless and harder – I wouldn't use the word 'dirty' but I'd say we had to be smarter, fighting at the right time. In 2010, our attitude was that we were going to be really hard to beat.

THE ACTION

★★★★★

WHEN BERNARD BROGAN – who would go on to win Footballer of the Year – struck for a goal in the first minute, it buoyed the large Dublin following. By half-time, the lead was four points, 1-8 to 0-7 but Cork lost inspirational captain Graham Canty to injury, with dual player Eoin Cadogan summoned in his place.

The introduction of Nicholas Murphy in the second half helped Cork to get a foothold in midfield, though the four-point still pertained with 17 minutes left. They got a break when another sub, Colm O'Neill, was fouled for a penalty just after his arrival. Greeted with a chorus of boos, Donncha O'Connor sent Stephen Cluxton the wrong way with his low kick and it was a one-point game, 1-10 to 1-9.

A levelling score seemed to be out of Cork's reach, with Dublin sub Conal Keaney making it 1-13 to 1-11 with four and a half minutes left. A pair of Donncha O'Connor frees finally tied things up with two minutes of normal time left, and he was handed a chance to put his side in the lead for the first time after a heavy-duty tackle by Ross McConnell on Noel O'Leary; the Dublin midfielder's second booking.

O'Connor nailed the free for his fifth point, and in injury time sub Derek Kavanagh put the Rebels two ahead. Dublin would get one last chance, but Bernard Brogan put his intended delivery over the bar.

★★★★★

My first campaign was in 2001. I was called on to the squad by Larry Tompkins that summer as I had been playing well with Nemo Rangers and I had a good Munster under-21 final. It was a few weeks before the first Munster Championship game against Waterford and I was brought on that day. I never got a league campaign under my belt or anything, I was just thrown in at the deep end, but I was being brought on in the championship games and that was a great experience.

Nemo retained the county in 2001 and we went on a good run in the Munster and All-Ireland Championships, so I didn't get any league games and I was kind of forgotten about and didn't make the championship panel for 2002. I remember feeling quite disappointed at the time but, in reality, I was only beginning to become a strong club player, and 2001 was probably too soon for me and I could completely understand why.

I didn't get a league campaign either in 2003, as Nemo won the All-Ireland, but I was back in for the championship – unfortunately, it was a brief journey as were knocked out by June 7. We were well beaten by Limerick in the Munster Championship and then the first round of the qualifiers was very early. There were a few other matches on the day that we played Roscommon in Dr Hyde Park but nobody was knocked out of the All-Ireland before Cork that year.

That was the end of Larry, and Billy Morgan came in again for the 2004 season. Obviously, Billy commanded huge respect and he was able to unearth the likes of Donncha O'Connor and Ger Spillane and bringing them into the panel. After losing in 2003 in the way we did, it was almost cathartic in the way that we had to regroup and rebuild everything. Billy really addressed the sports psychology side of it and put in a massive effort in terms of physical conditioning, engaging with experts from UCD.

It took a few years for that to bear fruit but, towards the end of the decade, it almost became a cliché for people to say what a big, strong team Cork were. That all started in the pre-season leading into 2003 – the amount of work that went in can't be over-stated, not just in strength and conditioning, but things like movement and diet. For me, it was the biggest turning point for us. People really bought into it and drove our professionalism.

A year and a half later, we were in an All-Ireland semi-final, which, for Cork, was probably no great shakes because it's what's expected as a county. But if you had told me at the end of 2003 that I'd be in an All-Ireland semi-final in 2005, I'd have been a bit sceptical.

We made big progress quite quickly but, hand in hand with that, we quickly became the source of people's frustrations: 'F**k it, ye lost an All-Ireland semi-final to Kerry?' I think, in hindsight, in 2005 and '06 we weren't ready to be a top-two, top-three team. By 2007, we were at that level, which is why the performance against Kerry in that year's final was such a disappointment and a sense of under-achievement.

I was captain in 2006 and '07 – I was the last captain under the old system where the county champions got to choose who got the job. I was happy to serve, but I didn't think that that was serving the team right. The county side had become a lot more of a regular team and the practice of a club nominating a captain was a generation old, from when you were picked to represent your county. It had all shifted in the 90s, or even the 80s, when county teams became more independent in their own right.

Billy's term ended after the 2007 final. When picking any management group, you have to have an element of autonomy and respecting the process. Cork County Board were obviously well within their rights to name a new manager and Teddy Holland, who I had good time for, possibly could have been a great manager. But the caveat that he went in with – 'Oh, by the way, we're also picking the selectors for you' – wasn't acceptable.

If that had happened when Billy came back in 2003, we might have raised an eyebrow at it but wouldn't have had the solidarity or the maturity to say, 'No, that's not going to work'. By the end of 2007, we had come through four hard years, making progress each season. We all saw how hard-earned it was, in that we really put everything into it. Every aspect, from mental preparedness to physical conditioning – we put so much of our lives into it and we learned that even that wasn't enough, because we were still frustrated. We wanted to win an All-Ireland and we knew all the ingredients involved – if the autonomy of a manager to pick his backroom team would be taken away from him, that was going to set us back a huge amount. If Teddy Holland was coming in, he needed to be able to pick whoever he wanted to come with him.

Our interpretation of it was that this was being done for the wrong reasons. Why would you name a manager but not give him full control? Our attitude was, after the effort we had put in, best of luck to them if they wanted to do that. We weren't going to commit for two or three years to a regime that we knew was doomed to fail. If you don't have the trust in above, it's just not going to work.

We all spoke together and the prevailing view was that there was no way we were going to put our lives on hold and put that level of commitment into something when the structure was so fundamentally wrong. Unfortunately, I think that Teddy got caught in the cross-fire of that.

Cork football had no obligation to me and, by the same token, I had no obligation to Cork football. There was no contract and I had every right to say that I didn't want to play. If someone else wanted to put up their hand and play, my view was that they didn't understand the background to the whole thing, but neither would I hold it against anyone.

To be honest, I did think there was a chance that our stance wouldn't work out and things would get too messy. We had dug our heels in so strongly and Cork County Board had dug their heels in; I didn't think anyone was going to back down. It was a very simple decision and if they went through the year without us, because they didn't respect our position, so be it. Thankfully, there was a resolution and Conor Counihan was the man chosen to take over.

I had great time for Conor. He had a slightly different brief to Billy in that the core panel was in place and it was a case of we were nearly there in terms of an All-Ireland, but still just short. We had to improve a bit in our physicality and our skills, but the mental toughness was the big thing. Conor had a much more refined task in that respect and he was absolutely brilliant at executing it.

He was coming into a group that might have been seen as difficult to work with after going on strike but he quickly established himself as the leader, no questions asked. Within minutes of meeting Conor, we knew that he was going to do his best for us, he was going to make us a better group and he wasn't going to tolerate any shit.

The 2009 All-Ireland final defeat to Kerry hurt big-time, because as a panel we were ready – so much so, that I couldn't even get into the team that year. I was having a lot of injuries but that team was performing at such a high level. The training that year was the best I've ever been exposed to; it was just frantic. Due to it being so high-pitched, I got injured a lot and couldn't get my place in the team as a result, but I can remember the pace and intensity. I really thought that we were going to win that 2009 final, especially given the manner of how the team had performed against Tyrone in the semi-final.

They were the All-Ireland champions and it was a physical statement as much as anything else, how we won that day. Kerry had come through the qualifiers but they were winning All-Irelands every second year during the 2000s so you can't say that we thought we were going to win 100 percent. We knew it was going to be a big battle, and it was – we felt that we had so many of the boxes ticked but they beat us.

We learned! Tadhg Kennelly should have been sent off at the very start but, more importantly, he should have been floored. Within seconds of him going for Nicholas Murphy, there should have been an all-out brawl and that's what we learned. It should have taken 10 minutes to clear up, there would have been one from each side sent off and that would have settled that. That's what we learned, and that's the edge that came into our training in 2010.

We were beaten in the 2010 championship, by Kerry after a replay in the Munster semi-final. The positive thing was that there was no dwelling on it. It didn't knock anything out of us. What happened was that, the first night we were back in training after that match, without anybody saying it, we went from fourth gear to fifth gear. The feeling was, *That competition is over now, we'll learn a little from it but now we're on to the next one and this is what we've been preparing for.* There was nothing to be gained by peaking too early and all of our physical training reflected the need to be at our best in August and September.

In 2002, Armagh changed the S&C landscape. They raised the bar completely. Their physical strength and sports science approach just changed the standard. When a team wins the All-Ireland, everybody takes a peek, but I think history will show that, when they won it, there was so much adopted from their practice. There was a big drive to bulk up and to bring a lot of science into the training area.

When Billy came in, he looked around at what was the best in the country and he used to bring us up to UCD. There was a guy, John Shuttleworth, and we loved him. He brought a big element of science to it and there was a huge improvement in us over a season or two. We all felt really good about our progress but it couldn't have happened without him, a professional coach. After that,

Conor Counihan brought in Aidan O'Connell, who was with Munster Rugby – again, a professional coach. We went from having amateur coaches to having professionals and our fitness, physique, all-round conditioning all improved.

I think every county team would say that from 2000, 2001... up to the end of the decade, the conditioning was light years apart, but the commentary around us was that we were so strong and so fit and we were definitely leading that.

In 2009, I had missed the entire National League, as I was away working. Due to Cork's form and my injuries, I couldn't get back into the team and the only game I featured in, believe it or not, was the All-Ireland final. I came on at the end… Kerry brought on Kieran Doherty and I was sent in to mark him.

I was only barely clear of injuries by then. It was August 2009 that I first had a diagnosis of the hip problem that would result in me having to get it replaced. I can remember physically crying after one training session that year, the feeling was, *My body's f**ked and I'm a mile away from this team.* I started to accelerate my own investigation into what was going on with my body and I found out that my hip was absolutely ruined. I got a cortisone injection and began to feel an immediate impact. I got closer and closer to the starting team.

One effect was that, yeah, I was frustrated that I wasn't starting, but it turned me into an angry competitor. I had the maturity to realise I was still part of it and it was for the team's greater good. I wanted to make sure that, if I got game-time, I was going to perform. Conor had a lot of us pissed off that we weren't starting, and eager to make an impression. When you think about it, that's what you want – 15 people really, *really* appreciating their position and knowing that, if they play badly, they're gone. Every team strives for that but we really got those ingredients right.

I never found it difficult coming into a game and getting to the pitch of it quickly. I looked at it from the point of view of being fighting fit and coming in with a half-hour or so left with my levels at 100 percent, to mark a guy who's half-spent. Nicholas Murphy and myself used to be regularly sprung from the bench – it might be Alan O'Connor and Pearse O'Neill coming off and we knew that the midfielders on the other side would be thinking, Oh, f**k this. I loved it!

I preferred playing in midfield compared to full-back from the point of view that you got to play a bit more of the ball. There was greater freedom and you got to express yourself more – catch high balls, take players on and generate scores – but I also loved playing full-back. You bring a different psyche to it, your game becomes a lot more focused – *All I have to do is spoil this fella.* The only thing you need to do is to be able to handpass the ball out of danger, whereas at midfield you're going to be kicking the ball 10, 20, 30 times, maybe even having to score a point, and there's a lot more thought goes into that.

You carried a lot less nervous tension playing at full-back and I loved the nature of it, the fight of it. Ultimately, I really didn't care as long as I was playing.

In 2008, Conor took us away from the Burlington and we actually stayed in Meath for our games in Croke Park. It was a place with a lot of pitches so we could work on things and it was quiet. In 2009, we went to Killiney and everything seemed to work out for us there. It was completely out of the way of supporters and it was a nice area.

We all had our little escape routines, such as going for a walk, but a lot of us got into the practice of going for a jump in the Forty Foot. That became a Saturday night ritual. A lot of us had been doing cold-water therapy as part of our recovery and here we had it on our doorstep. It was a beautifully scenic spot where you were jumping into the cold water the night before a big game, and it was brilliantly therapeutic and a great escape from the bubble of an All-Ireland semi-final or final. Staying in Killiney was a good fit for our team.

We had played Dublin a lot in challenge games around this time and it was noticeable that there was definitely a shift in them. They had been embarrassed by Kerry in 2009 and came back a lot stronger in '10. There certainly wasn't anyone looking past that game.

Bernard Brogan's goal was very early, so there was no panic. There was a real maturity in the team and we had been through so much. We knew we had a huge panel with five guys to come in if we needed it. We had been ahead in so many games and lost them, to know that we could do the opposite as well. Even the lead Dublin had in the closing stages, there was just an element of confidence and maturity in us. We had been through it all and you do really learn a lot from losing big games.

We prepared so well for that Dublin game. Even the crowd, which was the big unknown – we had obviously played in a full Croke Park before but we were being told that it was different to be playing in a full Croke Park against Dublin. We had Kevin Clancy as our sports psychologist at the time and he was very big into environmental impact, so he suggested dotting loudspeakers around Páirc Uí Chaoimh when we trained to replicate that deafening noise. As artificial as it sounds, that got us ready as well.

In a packed Croke Park, you're craning your neck to hear what's being said, and some messages aren't delivered properly and guys revert to type. With all the noise around us, we had to train to communicate in a more efficient way and that's how well-prepared we were for it.

I was brought on just after Donncha scored the penalty. Dublin had been up by five at one stage; the penalty brought it back to one, but they pushed it out to three again. It was such a rush to be involved… we had been dead and buried, but now we weren't and all of a sudden I was in the thick of it. I didn't have to provide a miracle – I didn't score goals and I wasn't being asked to do that, but I had to do my job and it was the same for Nicholas alongside me. At that point in our careers, there was very little going to intimidate us in terms of opponent or scoreline.

The All-Ireland final was my last game for Cork. Dr Éanna Falvey's advice in August 2009 had been to see out the year and then retire as my hip was in such a bad state. He administered a cortisone injection that day and I got a lot of relief from it. After the 2009 final, I went back to him and said, 'I hear what you're saying, but I want one more year'. We nailed it down, that I'd get an injection in around February, another in April/May and again in July. That would have to be it though, as my body was broken and a hip replacement was the only long-term solution. Regardless of what happen, 2010 was the last year.

It's funny, in a way: winning the All-Ireland felt like an anti-climax. I always remember losing on the big days and coming back into the dressing-room in Croke Park and thinking, *F**k it, it's just another pitch and just another game of football.* I had my A-game ready to go and I left it in the dressing-room. Why did I do that?

That's where sports psychology comes into it… and it is just another game. But then, you win in 2010 and the same is true… it's just another game. You're saying to yourself, *I thought there was going to be a different feeling, we ended the agony and all that,* but the lights go out pretty quickly, or they did for me anyway.

This had been my ambition from the age of nearly seven in 1987, when I started watching Cork play in All-Ireland finals. My number-one goal, above anything academic or professionally, was to win an All-Ireland with Cork. There's a lot of energy goes into that and 23 years later it happens – it can only be an anti-climax, and it was.

I'll always remember back in Cork by the Wednesday, people had moved on and Sunday was history… but of course it was. They're back doing their jobs – there was a bit of razzmatazz and a funny song on the radio coming up to the final and people wanted tickets and it was a good escape but, really, people don't care deeply beyond that. Bar a couple of die-hard supporters that would go to the training sessions and you know you had made a profound difference to their lives but, by and large, Joe Soap in the street didn't care.

That's the same for hurling too, by the way – there's an expectancy from the guy in the street that Cork will get to a hurling final, win it… and it'll be forgotten about by the Wednesday. The thing is, if you lose, they're not forgetting about it! That's the expectancy that's there in Cork.

I was out of it in 2011 and I felt sorry for the lads. They lost to Mayo in an All-Ireland quarter where Daniel Goulding, Colm O'Neill and Ciarán Sheehan were all out injured. They were three of the top forwards in the country and no team in Ireland could cope with that.

I think 2012 was the big one for Cork. They had enough expertise, enough youth and enough maturity to win that year. I walked away from Croke Park disappointed that Cork didn't beat Donegal in the All-Ireland semi-final, and the county hasn't got near that level of closeness to an All-Ireland final since then.

It's easy to say in hindsight that there was a determination that we would get it over the line in 2010, but there was. I remember reading the book *Legacy*, about the All Blacks and how they had an over-arching theme each year: for 2011, when they finally won the Rugby World Cup, their theme was 'Burn the Boats', stemming from the Spanish invasion of South America and no going back. Believe it or not, 'Burn the Boats' was the theme we had identified at the start of 2010 and revisited throughout the year.

But then, teams have those ambitions in every sport, every year, and it's kind of trite to say that you weren't going to be beaten. Every team can be beaten. When you think about it, we were taken to extra time by Limerick in the All-Ireland qualifiers and were very nearly beaten by Dublin the semi-final. What it was, was that we were going to maximise our ability to not be beaten and I think we did that. By 2010, we were at the stage where we didn't plan anything for September because we knew we were going to be in an All-Ireland final. That's how sure we were.

★ ★ ★ ★ ★

PAUL KERRIGAN

66

I WAS UNDER-21 for three years, 2005-07 – and I was captain for the first two of them, but not the third!

Nemo had won the county in 2004 and '05 and the rule was still in place that the champions had the captaincy the following year. We won Munster in each of the three years but it wasn't until 2007 that we won the All-Ireland.

Ken O'Halloran, Ray Carey, Michael Shields, Eoin Cadogan, Fintan Goold and Daniel Goulding were all on my age, and Steve O'Donoghue and Andrew O'Sullivan were two others who were on the senior panel for a time. When we came out of minor, there was a load of us playing under-21 straightaway, staying there for the three years, and obviously we were all part of the All-Ireland-winning squad. The year above us was Pa Kelly, Alan O'Connor, Paul O'Flynn and John Hayes, but I don't think there were many from the year above that went on to senior.

In 2003, we had got to the All-Ireland minor semi-final – we played very well against Galway in the quarter-final but then we lost to Dublin, and we didn't feel like we played well. The following year, we had a very good team but we lost to Kerry after a replay in Munster and then lost to Laois after a replay in the All-Ireland quarter-finals.

It was very hard to get on the Cork senior panel. I never lost a Munster under-21 game and we won the All-Ireland, but I still didn't get on the panel properly until the next year. Pa Kelly was a year older than me and it was similar for him. Fintan and Shieldsy were on it first, then Goulding got on it, so I was always asking them what it was like? When you got there, it really felt like you had earned your place.

I settled into playing at that level a bit easier, maybe – I was older and I had the conditioning done. I knew a few of the lads and we were fairly successful with Nemo, so I was going well at club level and at under-21. I had served my time before getting my chance, so I was in a position to be able to take it.

In 2007, they played an A-versus-B game just before the final and I was brought in to make the numbers. I only came on for five minutes towards the end – it was the game where Anthony Lynch broke his wrist, which caused him to miss the final.

We got to the All-Ireland club final with Nemo in 2008 – unfortunately, we lost to St Vincent's from Dublin. Conor Counihan had come into the job, and he and the management team were watching us in games in the Sigerson and with Nemo. Cork had to give walkovers for the first three league matches, but they staved off relegation.

After losing the All-Ireland, Nemo's first championship game of 2008 was four weeks later, on a Friday night against Aghada, and on the Sunday was Cork's last National League game, up in Crossmaglen against Armagh. I was in the bar in Nemo on the Saturday and the phone rang – myself and Brian O'Regan from Nemo were after being called up as there were a lot of players missing, and we were to go up on the train the following day.

I used to go to every game, up for weekends in Dublin and everything, so I knew all the players without knowing them… as a supporter, basically! I was down to room with Nicholas Murphy but he hadn't got the train up, and was driving up himself later. I was nervous and asked Derek Kavanagh to swap with me, so I went with Regan!

I was in the panel after that, but I was half-thinking about going to America for the summer. I had a few buddies that were going but I can remember talking to Peadar Healy, who was the coach at the time, and saying that I might travel but he was saying to hang on. Then I ended up making the panel and coming on late in the Munster final against Kerry, and scored a point.

We had the All-Ireland quarter-final against Kildare after that, but I didn't come on and I didn't come on in the drawn All-Ireland semi against Kerry, but I did come on in the replay, which we lost.

In the winter of 2008-09, I put in a big effort on the weights as it was my first real go at it. CIT won the Sigerson in 2009 too and we were going fairly well in the league – we were in Division 2, but we won it. I got in for the opening championship match down in Waterford and managed to stay there after that.

We probably should have won down in Killarney in 2009 – or at least we played well enough to win – but we beat Kerry well in the replay. We played poorly in the Munster final against Limerick but came out on top; then we hammered Donegal. Tyrone in the semi-final was a massive one. I can't remember who said it afterwards – I think it was one of the backroom guys – but you could sense on the Thursday night beforehand that we were going to put in a performance. We played a 10-minute game and it was electric… really, and it carried on into the game.

To beat them was a big one. I had grown up through the 2000s and I was a big fan of that team, and Kerry never managed to beat them. I remember being confident going in and it was one of our best performances and one of the most memorable games I was involved in. It was massive, really – winning an All-Ireland semi against the All-Ireland champions. They had won three and it was a team full of guys you'd look up to, so it was unreal.

Then, we were beaten by Kerry in the final. It was a funny one, because we probably played better football that year than we did in 2010. For four of the forwards, it was the first time starting in an All-Ireland final. We were young and some people might have put it down to that inexperience but for the older lads it was another final defeat. It was disappointing because we were favourites going into it. We got a great start, Colm O'Neill got a goal, but we ended up losing by four… and it felt like more than four. We just didn't play well at all, bar that first 10 minutes.

We were staying in the Burlington. On the Monday, before we got on the bus to get the train down to Cork, Conor Counihan called a meeting. He laid it down in front of us… 'Look, the final is over now, let's just get through the next few days and we're going to be back here next year'.

We were always going to be in contention if we played well, as we had a very good team at the time. At the start of 2010, we had a meeting and discussed a couple of things about the final – were we over-confident, had we prepared well, what did do we do well and what didn't we do well? But then it was about driving on from there.

We won the league in 2010, and would go on to win it again in '11 and '12. In 2010 and '11, we were only just back from the team holiday before the start, so it's not as if we were going bald-headed to win the competition. We used to rarely lose at home and when we went up north we did okay too. We had a lot of fellas who had been around the block and a lot of talented young fellas coming through.

When you've a good team, it's a lot easier to blend in younger lads – throw one in a line or whatever – and I think we were nearly built for Croke Park around then, it suited us, so we were confident in the league finals. To win three in-a-row was a good achievement, even if the usual thing you get – in Cork and nationally – is that it was *only* the league, but it was very competitive at the time. In 2010, we won the league and the All-Ireland, and then won the league again in '11, so that was three national titles in-a-row. We weren't really targeting the league in particular but once we got there, we wanted to win it, obviously.

We had Kerry in the Munster semi-final in 2010 and it was another draw in Killarney. We always felt that we could match them when we went out. We'd beat them generally in the Páirc, come close to them in Killarney and then, obviously, we struggled in Croke Park against them. We always took going to Killarney on its merits, that Cork hadn't won there in a while and that's what we wanted to do. We almost got used to drawing there and then having to go again a week later!

As a group, winning there was something we wanted to tick off and we weren't able to get over the line with that – I suppose you could say that a part of the Kerry mentality was that nobody wanted to be part of the team that got beaten by Cork in Killarney… or Croke Park! You have to bear in mind too that we were going up against one of the best teams to ever come out of Kerry.

We didn't play very well in the replay, but we were still ahead. Then Marc Ó Sé got a wonder-point to bring it to extra time and they had a bit more composure. It was disappointing –but at the same time it was probably a kick up the backside for us.

After the Kerry game, I think there was a round of club games and I can remember being up watching a session at Collins Barracks, and it was a right tough one for the boys that were training. There was a great attitude – you could see that fellas were really disappointed but they just had the heads down, wanting to work hard. We hit the road after that.

We had Cavan at home first and they weren't great. We had a couple of injuries

– I actually missed that game – and it was probably a good draw. First game out, you want to be at home and they were a couple of divisions below us, not as strong then as they are now. It was a fairly miserable day down the Páirc and it probably set us for the next match, a right tough battle away to Wexford.

The conditions were very tough that day and we only just came out of it. It felt like a real championship game, with a good crowd at it and it felt like every game was setting us up for the next one. Wexford was a tough game… and that set us up for the next one, away to Limerick. They had been unlucky not to beat Kerry in the Munster final and they took us to extra time but we got through it.

I remember after that match, being in the hotel and it felt like a small bit of a breather – we had made it back to Croke Park – even though the Roscommon match was a week later again. When we beat them, it felt like we had a good, tough month put down; we were able to take a bit of a break and then prepare for the semi-final against the Dubs, which was three weeks later.

The day before the Roscommon game, Dublin had beaten Tyrone in the quarter-finals and Kerry had been knocked out by Down. We were going up on the bus and listening to it on the radio – rather than watching it on the phone, like you would be now! – and the big immediate takeaway was that the two favourites had been beaten and we had to make sure it didn't happen to us. We were probably beyond any complacency at that stage, but we were just going to make sure that we weren't caught either.

For a game in Dublin, we'd always head up the day before. We'd meet up in Rochestown Park Hotel and get the bus from there. At that time, we were staying in the Fitzpatrick Castle Hotel in Killiney and it was unbelievable. In 2009, we had stayed at Johnstown Estate in Enfield. What became a tradition in Killiney for a dozen of us was, the night before the game, to go down to the Forty Foot and jump in! It started with Alan Quirke and Derek Kavanagh… and then a few more of us started doing it. It was nice to do something in the evening.

I used to room a lot with Pearse O'Neill in 2009 – Conor used to do this thing where an older fella would be looking out for a younger guy, and Pearse was my 'mentor' for the year. I think I was rooming with Pa Kelly in 2010 as we were both wing-forwards. Aidan O'Connell, our strength and conditioning coach, would have been big on getting a good sleep in early on the night before a match but I wouldn't usually be a great sleeper in hotels anyway – I tried not let it bother me, though. I was used to that situation from away league games and stuff, so I didn't worry about it.

On the morning of a game, I used to be very nervous and I still would be, even before a Nemo match. I'd go down for breakfast and maybe get a rub, hang around the games room – trying to take the mind off the game, but the mind wouldn't be off it! You're just waiting for the game to come.

I used to sit next to Fintan Goold on the bus for those years, something that we did in 2009 and just kept going. Our psychologist at the time, Kevin Clancy, used to have a video that he would put on maybe halfway through the journey – highlights of good things we had done and special moments – and that was intended as a final kicker. By the end of his time with us, around 2012, that became the thing fellas were waiting for on the bus!

Bernard Brogan got the goal in the first minute of the 2010 semi-final, but nobody was panicking. We were always a team who created a lot of opportunities, even though our conversion rate wasn't always the best. Bernard was on fire that year and it was a big ball over the top and an unbelievable finish, but we had a lot of steady fellas on the team and it was just going to be about the next ball.

Our bench was huge that year. Derek Kavanagh and Nicholas Murphy used to come on and finish the game in midfield, then Colm O'Neill and John Hayes would come on in the forwards… and we had good backs too. We had a big thing about our panel and the level of fitness we had built up, so the goal was an inconvenience, but nobody was worried. We didn't play particularly well but we were still only the goal down at half-time and our conversion rate was shocking. We were there or thereabouts, still.

At the time, Dublin had a fairly young team and we used to beat them regularly. We had beaten them by seven points in the league in 2010 and we gave them some awful hidings in challenge games, sometimes not even with full teams. They were a good Division 1 team, but they weren't on the radar like Tyrone or Kerry would have been. We respected them as they were a coming team, but there was definitely no fear.

That year, I used to wear No 10 and Pa was No 12, but we played the opposite sides, for some reason. Then, if Ciarán Sheehan was playing, he'd often be on the left wing and I'd be inside in the corner. Against Dublin, I had Philly McMahon marking me and I did actually end up in the No 10 for the last quarter. Kevin Nolan picked me up then.

Philly was aggressive and mouthy, but he was good on the ball too and he got a point that day. I felt that I could do well on him if I got a bit of space… and I got a good point off him in the first-half. I hit the crossbar too and I definitely felt I was a match for him in the one-on-one stakes. At that level, it's easy enough to ignore any sledging, especially as it's so loud in a full Croke Park, and there isn't even a whole pile of it as fellas have enough to be worrying about. You probably get more at club level.

We had two very good free-takers in Donncha and Goulding, and myself and Pearse were strong runners at defences so we won a lot of frees. Even if you weren't fouled, you might carry it in and give it to them on the loop. I would be targeting a couple of points but I felt that my main job was to take the fight to the opposition backs, put them on the back foot and take them on. When the ball was around the midfield or half-back line, my role was to get us up the field. The two lads were the heavy scorers, but the rest of us – myself, Pa, Pearse, Fintan, Ciarán or whoever else – would chip in with one or two too.

Dublin did respond after Donncha scored the goal from the penalty but we really got on top then. The period from the 60th minute on felt like it went slowly for us and it probably went quickly for Dublin. We got a couple of frees – maybe some were a bit handy – but we had no better lads to tip them over.

The great sign of the squad was the bench. We lost Graham in the first-half to injury and that might have knocked us in the past as he was such a leader, but we absorbed it. Derek and Nicholas came on and made a difference, and Colm came on, scored a point and won the penalty. I had no doubts whatsoever that Donncha would stick the penalty. I had seen him take them at club level and in training – regardless of who was in goal, he always scored.

We were a good team to come back. Often, we found ourselves trailing by a lot against Kerry but came back to draw or just lose by a point. We had it in us. Noel O'Leary was fouled for the free that Donncha scored to put us ahead and, once we were ahead, I felt that we weren't going to be beaten.

Beating Dublin like that was probably a help in getting over Down in the final. We probably didn't realise how big a win the Dublin game was until after it. You were meeting people who were saying, 'It was an incredible atmosphere'…

and even to this day it's one that I'm asked about. Even the parade that day, for example, was a great experience. It was electric.

I was definitely confident that we would win. We probably didn't play well for the entire year but we were getting the results, and that's the way it panned out as well for the final. One thing from the final that might have gone unnoticed by most is that, after Graham Canty lifted the Sam Maguire, Shieldsy was next as he was vice-captain and led us out that day and went up for the toss as Graham started the bench. After them were all the subs… and it underlined how it had been a supreme squad effort, and the unity and mutual respect there was huge.

My father Jimmy and I are the only Cork father and son with All-Ireland senior football medals since 1945 – it wasn't something that occurred to me until a good few years afterwards.

I can't remember my dad playing with Cork at all. He was 27 when I was born in December 1986, and he retired after the '91 championship – he had been playing with Cork since '79. I wouldn't have big on watching videos of old games and the only ones I looked at where he was involved was the Compromise Rules in 1984 and '86. I was half-obsessed with that game, I liked the concept and there was plenty of fighting! We ended up being the second father-son pairing to represent Ireland in that, after Kerry's Seán and Tommy Walsh.

Obviously, I was aware of what he had done and people would talk a lot about him. Even though he played his best football as a back, I was always a forward – in Gaelic anyway, as I was a centre-half in soccer! Starting off, I was a corner-forward and then as a teenager I had a growth spurt and became very quick, so I was used more in the half-forward line.

It was a double-edged sword, having a father that had achieved so much. Expectations were raised and if things weren't going well with Cork or Nemo, you'd wouldn't get a telling-off exactly, but you'd know that improvement was needed! On the other hand, when I came into the Cork panel first, I remember Alan Quirke saying, 'We've a Kerrigan now, that's a good-luck charm!'

When my own son, Billy was born, a colleague said to me that, as tough as I had it, he was going to have it twice as bad in terms of expectations!

99

GRAHAM CANTY
(& DANIEL GOULDING)

CORK 0-16 ★ DOWN 0-15
All-Ireland SFC Final
Croke Park
SEPTEMBER 19, 2010

★ **CORK:** A Quirke; E Cadogan, M Shields, R Carey; N O'Leary, J Miskella, P Kissane; A O'Connor, A Walsh; C Sheehan (0-1), P O'Neill, P Kelly; **D Goulding (0-9)**, D O'Connor (0-5), P Kerrigan (0-1). **Subs:** N Murphy for O'Connor, **G Canty** for Kissane, C O'Neill for P O'Neill, D Kavanagh for Murphy, J Hayes for Kerrigan, F Goold for Kavanagh.

★ **DOWN:** B McVeigh; D Martin, D Gordon, D Rafferty; D Rooney, K McKernan (0-1), C Garvey; P Fitzpatrick (0-1), K King; D Hughes (0-3), M Poland (0-1), B Coulter (0-1); P McComiskey (0-3), J Clarke (0-1), M Clarke (0-3). **Subs:** C Maginn for J Clarke, R Murtagh (0-1) for McComiskey, B McArdle for Rafferty, A Brannigan for King, C Laverty for Poland.

66

THERE WAS NEVER a stage in my youth when there was a Eureka moment that I had the potential to play for Cork. Basically, you played for Cork under-16s, a couple of years minor... and then on to under-21. Up to senior in the last year under-21, played away and then you were finished!

In more realistic terms, you never stopped to think, *Wow, I'm playing at a high level here.* You just played what was in front of you... the next game, the next year. That's not to say that there wasn't goal-setting or anything, but it was more in terms of recognising the weaknesses to work on and strengths to capitalise on.

Bantry Blues had won the county intermediate championship in 1993, which was a huge thing when you're an impressionable 12- or 13-year-old, going to the games with your family. They went on to win the senior in 1995 and there was a

THE ACTION

★★★★★

THE REBELS COULD have had a dream start had Down goalkeeper Brendan McVeigh not denied Ciarán Sheehan. Instead, the opening stages were even, but after Daniel Goulding converted a second free to level in the 13th minute, Cork would not score for another 17, as Down really began to assert themselves.

Martin Clarke would score three frees in this time as they went five clear, 0-7 to 0-2. However, Cork managed to stem the tide as the interval neared, powerful running by Paul Kerrigan and Aidan Walsh resulting in scores for Goulding and Donncha O'Connor, and there was just three in it as the sides turned around, 0-8 to 0-5 for Down.

The introduction of Canty lifted Cork, and two frees by Daniel Goulding had the gap at two, 0-9 to 0-7, by the 44th minute. There was one point in it with 22 minutes left. Sheehan tied the game up, but Down centre-back, Kevin McKernan put them back in the lead.

Cork were a transformed side, though, and Donncha O'Connor levelled again before Kerrigan's first point had them in front for the first time since the early stages. They were allowed some breathing space as a pair of excellent Goulding '45s' made it 0-14 to 0-11.

The game came down to one point, but when the need was greatest, Cork were composed. A brilliant kick-out from Quirke was won by sub Fintan Goold and they finished the game on the attack.

★★★★★

huge buzz in the town at the time, to see the team competing hard at a high level. You wanted to play senior football for Bantry.

As well, you'd go to a lot of Cork-Kerry games, and Ciarán O'Sullivan was someone from whom I took a lot of inspiration. He was an attacking wing-back who could score and defend. He was aggressive, he was fearless and, of course, he was from back down West as well. He was a good footballer, fit and strong, up and down the pitch and a ferocious clubman for Urhan… and gave his all for Beara. The fact he came from a small club showed that you didn't have to be from a big, huge club to make it, once you had that bit of drive. There were so many fellas like that on the Cork team that won the All-Irelands under Billy Morgan and anybody who had any interest in football knew them all – even without the level of media coverage that you have now.

I was lucky enough that there were a few people at home with Bantry that looked after me. Dr Denis Cotter, who passed away in recent years, sent me to Wolfe Tone Park one day when I was still only 15… 'The seniors are training; they're all doing weights and you'll do weights too'. I went away out and met Seánie McGrath, who would later be involved with the Cork hurlers as a strength and conditioning coach. I told him Cotter had sent me and he took one look at this scrawny 15-year-old and said, 'Yeah, we'll put you on a programme, but you won't be doing what the lads are doing'. I lifted no weights that winter – it was more flexibility and mobility, time on the exercise bike and the rower, but I was falling in with the senior lads for the core stuff. Seánie would give me one or two things to work on each week and it progressed from that.

Cork struggled in my two years at minor. In the first year, 1997, there was just one game, a Munster semi-final loss to Kerry. We lost to Limerick in my second year – that Limerick side came and they came hard. They were a good side and we weren't good enough on the day. At under-21, we won Munster in my final year, but the All-Ireland semi-final against Tyrone was delayed due to Foot and Mouth disease, and they hockeyed us – seven or eight of them went on to win senior All-Irelands.

I had been tipping around the senior panel in 2000. It was noticeable how much less time you had on the ball at senior level. I can remember playing a league game away to Galway, winning a couple of breaks and fouling the ball for over-carrying as I was put under pressure straightaway. It was about making decisions quicker, and being more aware of what was around you. When you won the ball, you had to have some kind of plan… a get-out-of-jail card, you had to be smarter and cuter. At that level, you don't think, you just *do* and that comes with experience.

At the start, I was often put in the full-back line, but I never minded it – you'd fill any old gap at all once you'd be kept. We won Munster in 2002, and then in '03 I missed the first championship match, the loss to Limerick, as I was doing college exams. People talked about it as being a big call or a brave one, but it was easy enough, really. I wasn't prepared enough and I wasn't going to be able to perform to a level where I'd be able to do anything for the team. I felt I wasn't a good enough asset to the team at the time to be at 80 percent capacity – I felt I had to be operating in the high 90s to be able to contribute. What took priority was trying to fall over the line in my final year in college! Larry Tompkins was very supportive and very approachable with the whole thing – early on in the year, when I said it to him, he said we could play it by ear and he was understanding when I missed sessions. You remember that when you're under the cosh.

I was back for the game against Roscommon in the qualifiers, but we lost that and the season was over early. It proved to be Larry's last year as Billy Morgan returned. Billy was great to believe in his players – you might be looking over the border or up north and thinking some fella is a great centre-back, but Billy would be telling you, you were the best in the country and you'd believe it! He demanded high standards of us as a group and got a good team around him.

He bought in massive to strength and conditioning, supported by diet and recovery, getting that mix right. Whoever you were on the panel, whether you were number 1 or 30, the same was expected of everyone and that was the culture he set. The results mightn't have followed immediately, but it was always enjoyable.

After losing to Fermanagh in the qualifiers in 2004, we began to get on a roll. We reached the All-Ireland semi-finals in 2005, and then beat Kerry after a replay in '06 but I tore my cruciate in that game and I was out for eight or nine months. I never had any fears about not making it back – or nothing that I'd ever have admitted to myself, anyway!

Looking at it rationally, I knew that loads of people had gone through it and all I had to do was get the operation done by a top surgeon – Tadhg O'Sullivan did it in Waterford – and work with our physio Colin Lane, who I was seeing nearly every day of the week for a while! There was a very structured, rigid plan and I never asked Colin to let me see the whole thing or what it involved… I was happy to tick the boxes and inch forward. We moved to the next stage when I was ready; not when any plan on the internet said you should be ready.

Gradually, I came back to training and playing, but there was a lot of frustration then when you realise… you're shit! The one thing Colin couldn't sort was match-fitness – once he gave the green light, you were ready and fully able to play, but it was case of getting minutes under your belt wherever you could to get the rustiness out of you.

I was back for 2007, when we made the All-Ireland final but were well beaten by Kerry. It's funny… even when things weren't going well, at the start of every year you believed you could win an All-Ireland. You might have lost a semi-final in Munster the year before and the group wouldn't have changed much, but you still believed and had to *believe*. That's probably what helped us get to the final in 2007 – we did well to get there, we didn't win it but you just bank it and move on, see where the inches are that you could improve again.

It's well known what happened off the field in the wake of that – the bottom line was that there were no winners in what went on. Billy moved on but everything else went, when there would have been a lot of benefits from having continuity. Obviously, we ended up going on strike and it was tough going.

We were a tight-knit group and we felt that we didn't have any other choice. We wanted to do what was right… put on the jersey and represent Cork properly, be well-enough prepared that, when you went to Páirc Uí Chaoimh or Páirc Uí Rinn or wherever and a crowd came to watch you, you had a chance of winning. It was an easy decision from that point of view and it probably did galvanise us another bit.

We were a very diverse group in terms of experience and age and so on, but the opinion was unanimous and it was easy to move forward as a group. I say 'forward' – for a lot of the time it felt like we were going nowhere, and that that was the end of our Cork careers. That was a tough prospect, but we were willing to let it there because we believed in what we were doing.

Eventually, when matters were resolved, Conor Counihan was appointed and he brought a really good team with him the first day we met him above in Páirc

Uí Rinn. Most of them were really under-stated and a lot of people wouldn't know who they are, even to this day, but Conor brought in a strong set-up and even improved it as the years passed.

When Conor came in, he made me captain. I didn't even think about it – I just got on with things. It was great, obviously, and nice to be asked but it wasn't something I dwelled on a whole lot. When we returned from the strike, there was a lot of work to do in terms of catching up with every other team and we were trying to hang on to our Division 2 status, so there were more important things to be thinking about!

The cliché with a lot of sides is that there's a team of captains, but it really was like that with us. Some of that happened naturally, but Conor would have done work on it too, identifying leaders in different areas of the pitch. When it came down to it, the captaincy meant going up for the toss and if there were any cups to be got, you were the first person to get your hands on it! Other than that, all of the leadership came from the group and you were part of that group. If you thought it was anything other than that, Conor would set you right – or one of the lads in the group would.

We won Munster in Conor's first year, but lost to Kerry after a replay in the All-Ireland semi-final. They were probably still ahead of us then but in 2009 we beat them in a replay in Munster and then beat Limerick in the Munster final. We made it to the All-Ireland final again… and Kerry beat us. Given that we had played so well for so much of that year, it was tougher to take than the 2007 defeat had been.

The squad was stronger and we had good form going into it. It was tough to take, obviously, but it was always the case that, no matter how you'd done the previous year, you dusted yourselves down and went again. I can remember Dr Con Murphy asking me once what we'd have done if we hadn't won the All-Ireland in 2010… and I just said it would have been the same thing, win or lose – you face into the new season. There was never a guarantee you were going to win every year but you were going to go as hard as you could, with a plan in place, and see how far it brought you. Maybe that sounds a bit too simplified but that's how it felt in my head.

We lost to Kerry in a replay in the Munster semi-final in 2010, but nobody was panicking. We were used to playing Kerry – we were used to beating Kerry, we were used to losing to Kerry. They were two good teams and we came out on the wrong side of it on the day. I was sent off for two yellow cards that day and that was frustrating but, you know what, I might have got away with a couple of double-yellows at other times in my career! It's small margins but you get on with it and that's what we did.

Cavan was the first game in the qualifiers, down the Páirc, and we were too strong for them. Then we had Wexford away and we won by 0-12 to 0-5 – people might look at it and think it was comfortable, but that was a tough game. Forty minutes into the game, we were struggling, but we found a way to win and it was the same in the next match, away to Limerick.

At the time, there was a bit of coverage around how Cork could be playing a better style of football, but that was fairly easy to shut out. I'd always maintain that we had a good style of football but at the same time you're going to be looking at the opposition and not being naïve enough to just play away. You're always slightly changing how you set up or which personnel play where or what you do. The bottom line was that it was knockout football and you were trying to win the games. We had very good players and a very good management team, and the lads in the group cared more about winning than how we won – but we still played good football, I thought! You'd hear stuff a particular player… 'wasn't being allowed to play' but if you talked to any of those players, they had no issues.

The group definitely got stronger and by 2010 the squad had so many top-quality players that the management were able to make the most of that. If a player wasn't fully fit, say, he could be kept back to be used as a sub, or even until the next game, because there was somebody just as good capable of starting.

We were lucky with the lads that Conor had brought in for video analysis; they did the prep-work for you in terms of who you'd be marking in the next game. You'd sit down with them and discuss things, but we'd discuss it as a group as well. You'd know who you'd be detailed to be on and sometimes if they were going to play at 13, 14, 11 or whatever, you'd follow them; other times, it might be the case that you'd follow them across 10, 11 and 12, but not if they went into the full-forward line. It varied depending on the opposition, depending on what we wanted to play or how we wanted to play. Some days it worked and some days it didn't.

I tore my hamstring against Roscommon in the All-Ireland quarter-final. It was a fairly bad tear and I struggled with it until the semi-final against Dublin, where I hurt it again. I had to come off at half-time and then, basically, it was a race against time to see if I could get it right for the final.

There was obviously a fear that I wouldn't make it. I was checking in with Dr Con and Colin, probably every day since the quarter-final… and all the way to the final. You'd take three steps forward and then maybe one step back – which wouldn't be a huge problem normally but now you had the same end-date. Coming back from the cruciate, I used to always be asking Colin when I could play a game and he'd reply, 'When it's ready – you'll know yourself'. The All-Ireland final date was set and any setback made it harder and harder to be ready for it.

It was easy enough for Colin and Dr Con to know that I wouldn't be able to play the full game and then, three or four days before the final, it was a case of determining how I'd be able for coming off the bench. The rationale was to bring me on early enough that, if it did blow up, so be it… and somebody else could come in again. We didn't want it to happen so late that there were no subs left.

Leading up to the final, I was having to do a lot of rehab work on my own, so I was remote from the group for a lot of it. Obviously, I wanted to be there to support the group as much as I could, but I had to get myself right so I was nearly isolated from them. It was great, then, to have so much support from people back in Bantry. They'd never give you a call when things were going well – they'd feel they might be bothering you and would just let you alone! – but there were a few who you could rely on to lift your spirits, and even a few who had passed away by then who used to be similar, who you were also thinking about.

When the team was named for the final, I was at centre-back wearing No 6, even though everyone in the camp knew that I wouldn't be starting. There wasn't too much to contend with in the way of meeting people and having to let on – I didn't have to interact with the public in my job and, while there were a few in the office who'd talk football, they'd let you alone the week of a final anyway.

When I was much younger, I used to worry if I didn't sleep well the night before a game but during Larry's time in charge, I remember him telling us about not sleeping a wink the night before a match, and going out and having a stormer. A football match was only going to last 70 or 80 minutes, so you'd have enough in the tank for that, whether you slept well or not – the irony was that, because I wasn't worried about sleeping well, I usually slept like a log anyway before a match!

The roommates varied. Conor never said that you'd always be paired with X, Y or Z. I roomed a bit with Donncha, Pearse O'Neill and Michael Shields. The hotel in Killiney was perfect for us and below in the basement was a games room, with a big meeting room off it. You'd be messing around there, playing table tennis or darts or whatever, or you might go for a walk – so you didn't spend much time in the room anyway.

Cork had obviously lost two of the previous three finals, but I never thought beforehand, *Christ, if we lose this one it'll be a total disaster.* It would have been unbelievably disappointing, just like any other loss, but there was a big prize there to be played for.

I had been lucky enough to have started most games for Cork when I was available. There were some games where I had played zero but, generally, I wasn't togged for those so the build-up was a bit different when I was going to be a sub. It was a case of trying to make sure I was mentally right so that I could perform when I did come on.

Even the warm-up, most of the time you do it so that you're ready to go, but here you were going to be sitting on your ass again – the important thing was to help prepare the starting 15 so that they were *prepared.* During the first-half, I was sitting beside Colm O'Neill and that was great because he was as relaxed as anything, and he always is. He'd nearly have a running commentary on the game… 'Jesus Canty, if you'd been there, even you'd nearly have kicked that over!'… and that helped me to stay relax, too. At the time, Colm was a great impact sub, so you're saying to yourself, *If he's alright knowing that he's going to come on and contribute, I'm alright too.*

You were watching it, knowing that you were almost definitely going to be coming on in the half-back line – Conor was unlikely to throw me in alongside Goulding or anything! To that end, you're paying more attention to that area, what kind of ball Down were sending in, how we were doing from our own kickouts? You're trying to look at that objectively rather than kicking every ball – and knowing as well that you're not going to be at 100 percent when you do come on.

When the final whistle went, Benny Coulter was nearby. I would have known him from playing International Rules together and I had a lot of respect for him. I went over to him and sympathised, as it was a position I had been in so I knew how he felt. Then Alan Quirke was nearby too and we embraced, and it meant a lot that all of the group could come together, players and management, and savour it.

I didn't have any speech written beforehand. I met Dr Con on the way up and he asked me if I had anything prepared? When I said I hadn't, he said, 'I f**king knew you wouldn't!'… and he put a slip of paper into my hand and told me it'd keep me on the straight and narrow. He was always a step ahead, always looking out for you, whether it was medically or mentally – or secretarially in this case! I don't think I did read from it, but it was there as a crutch if I needed it.

After the homecoming in Cork on the Monday night, it was a real privilege to come to Bantry on the Tuesday and to introduce the group to the lads at home. There was an awful lot of preparation went into the night from the people in the club at home and it was only three or four years later that it dawned on me that the same planning had probably gone in in 2009, only for it to have to be thrown in the bin when Kerry beat us. For the club to put on that kind of show was a real honour

Winning was great, obviously, but if I was sitting here now without an All-Ireland medal, I don't think it would hugely bother me – it's not what I played football for. When I started off, my aim was to play senior for Bantry and the rest of it just kind of happened, to be honest. While you're in there, naturally you want to drive on and see where you can go with the group. Every year, you wanted to be able to say you gave it your best: you mightn't have done everything right, but you weren't left wondering.

We could have won an All-Ireland before 2010 and we could have won an All-Ireland after it, but Down were a whisker away from winning it in 2010. In 2011, we still had the ability to win games even when we weren't at our best but we got caught with a lot of injuries. And in 2012, we had added a couple of players and we were in good form, but we came up against a really good Donegal team in the semi-final and, on the day, we played alright but they were better than us. That happens.

The bond between that group was always strong and it has remained strong.

That was seen when Kieran O'Connor was diagnosed with cancer and sadly died in 2020. That was a savage tough time for Kieran and his family, but I wasn't surprised by the reaction of the group and it would be the same for any of us.

Ever before that, you'd have been proud to have been part of that group, with the way they conducted themselves on the pitch and off it, and that pride would be there even if we won nothing.

★ ★ ★ ★ ★

DANIEL GOULDING

66

YOU'D LIKE TO think that there wasn't a lot of pressure on us going into the 2010 final but, in hindsight, there was a huge amount. As well as having lost two finals, we were playing Down, who were a surprise package, meaning that we were heavy favourites.

In the camp, it was a case of trying not to acknowledge the pressure and focusing on it as just another game, but in the first-half, you could see it… it was there, subconsciously, in everybody's heads, *This is our big chance after losing two.*

I would have – and I know a lot of the other lads would have, too – done a lot of mental preparation, focusing on the game, but when you're alone with yourself, various thoughts come into your mind the whole time.

I had landed into the panel at the back-end of 2005 and started making the matchday squad during '06. The group from that point forward was made up of guys of Graham Canty's vintage – Nicholas Murphy, Anthony Lynch and those lads, who had soldiered for years with Cork without success – and then you had players of my age and John Hayes' age, who had won Munsters and All-Irelands at under-21, and there was a nice blend. Things generally clicked straightaway – the older lads led by example and set the culture, which the younger lads bought into. There was a nice balance there, developed by Billy Morgan in the first couple of years. It was year four or five for that group being together by 2010.

We had been away on holidays and training camps together, and it was a tight-knit group. Lads were well-versed in how to prepare for games and what was required if you were part of that panel.

In the spring of that year, we went on a character-building trip to Bere Island, training with the army. At the time, you'd have been cursing it. John Hayes wrote a diary of the week of the All-Ireland for the *Irish Examiner* and it was sent on to me a while back – he covered Bere Island and it was only reading back that I remembered how awful it was.

Jesus, it was brutal when you think of it. We were just absolutely dogged for two and a half days. Niall Twomey from Bantry, who has been involved with Cork underage squads, led it along with his army colleagues and it was severe. You wouldn't put it down as being the making of us, obviously, but it definitely helped the group and galvanised us a bit further. It was cruel, it was non-stop… and it kept asking questions of you. To be fair, unless a fella broke down injured, to a man everybody completed it.

There was some great fun there too and great memories; reading that diary John wrote, it was nice to look back and have a laugh at it but it was tough going at the time… especially for a fella like me, who doesn't like running anyway!

We had won Division 2 of the national league in 2009 and we followed that with the Division 1 title in '10. Aidan Walsh and Ciarán Sheehan were the big finds of the league and they were massive for us. Neither of them had any fear – or the scars from other years – and they took the game as they saw it. At the time, they didn't think about it too much, just turned up and played. When you're 19 in a set-up like that, everything's new to you and you just take it as you see it. They both made huge contributions throughout the season and especially in the final. Aidan was excellent in the middle of the field and Ciarán had a huge second-half. For two 19-year-olds to do that was really impressive.

In 2008 and '09, we had won the Munster title, but in 2010 we lost in the semi-final to Kerry after an extra-time replay in Páirc Uí Chaoimh. It meant we had to go through the qualifiers, but it wasn't a defeat that knocked the confidence out of us – we felt that we could have won that replay just as easily as lost it, it just came down to a few mistakes at critical times. We didn't have much time to reset, the qualifiers were a few weeks later and we got back on the road straightaway.

The first game was Cavan at home, they were going very poorly at the time so it was a nice way to settle back in with a good win.

After that, it's down to the luck of the draw and we got two away draws… against Wexford and Limerick. They were two very hard games and, while you wouldn't say we were lucky, we did very well to get out of the two of them with wins, because there were times where we came under a lot of pressure. That then gave you that bit of confidence and belief again that you could handle the bit of adversity and that, when the hard questions were asked of you, you could respond. Against Wexford in Wexford Park, we had played with a gale-force wind and were only two or three points up at half-time and we had to put in a huge performance in the second-half to get through.

The next day against Limerick, we could have crumbled after we were caught with a sucker-punch of a goal to send the game to extra time. We had serious battles with Limerick over the years and this was huge result, to get out of the Gaelic Grounds with a win after taking control again in extra time.

Then we were on to Roscommon in the All-Ireland quarter-final and we won that handy enough after a close first-half. Obviously, the semi-final and the final are the two games you'd remember most.

Obviously, the players and the management had a big role in the All-Ireland win but someone who probably doesn't get enough credit – and would never look for it – is Mick Curtin. He was in charge of the logistics, having started in Billy Morgan's first stint; he celebrated his 30th anniversary in 2023. He is always there and yet he goes totally unnoticed, which is an impressive thing in its own right.

In my time, he would do anything for you – the majority of the time, you wouldn't even have to ask. When you were playing a club championship match, he'd be at the gate afterwards with your protein shake.

It's mad when you think of it – you mightn't have seen Mick in a few weeks since the National League ended, and you went back to your club and next thing he's at your game with your recovery drink. And that was only for me; I presume he did it with everyone.

It just shows that he's so selfless, always thinking about the players. It's an incredible thing. It's hard to describe him but he's nearly saintly, always there and doing the right thing. Mick's capacity to do work and be prepared, with such attention to detail, meant every manager found him invaluable. He was just always on top of things. I remember back in the day, there was a while where we didn't even wash our own gear and you'd come to every training and whichever gear we were meant to be wearing was ready for you to go.

Mick must have been getting to training at 3 or 4 o'clock to get all of that organised, having been up early to do the post. Whoever was first there, you could be guaranteed that Mick would have been there an hour or two before them. He's held in such high regard and he's a great friend. There'll always be a Christmas card and then he'll randomly shoot you a text asking how you're getting on and wishing you the best for the championship.

That's fine if you think about it for one person, but Mick has dealt with hundreds of people over the last 30 years. I've no doubt he's on to a lot of people still and it just shows how conscientious and caring he is. Whether it was the good days or the bad days, you didn't know with Mick. He was always just encouraging you and keeping positive. I don't think I've ever heard Mick say anything negative.

It's always been about the task at hand and looking to the future... 'We'll sort it the next day.' It's an attitude that, if we could have all taken it on, you mightn't have had to worry about half the things you did worry about.

The day before the Roscommon game, Down had beaten Kerry and Dublin had knocked out Tyrone. We had been on the way to Dublin in the bus and were stopped at the Midway in Portlaoise when the news came in. The natural thing is to be a bit...relieved is probably not the word, but excited about the whole thing. In my mind, being honest, it definitely was a bit of a boost seeing Kerry gone but you have to very quickly bring yourself down to the fact that we had a quarter-final the following day to think about.

When it came down to it, Conor Counihan and the rest of the management were quick to dispel any idea that things would be easy – it was grand Kerry being gone, but we had to focus on Roscommon and make sure we wouldn't be *gone*. That was the good thing about having the older lads there like Graham and Alan Quirke; they were able to read a situation very quickly and everyone was back in line straightway.

While the defeats in the previous two finals meant we had the pressure mentioned earlier, those experiences definitely helped us in terms of preparing for the weekend of the final. In 2007, I took things at face value – everything was new and exciting and, anyway, I was a sub so I didn't have the responsibility of starting and everything was rosy in my head. By the time of the third final, we had learned to get all of the distractions out of the way two weeks out – suits, gear, all of that, everything was boxed away.

All you're doing then for the fortnight coming into it is training and recovering, trying to get away from it on the nights you're off, trying to hang with your friends or do something with your girlfriend to take your mind off the game. The build-up to the game can be tiring and, even the year previously, it was Cork-and-Kerry talk for three weeks solid beforehand. With Cork and Down, it's not constantly in your head from other people.

Obviously, Cork play in red and white, and Down are red and black, so both teams had to change jerseys for the final. I don't think there was any problem adjusting, I think fellas actually liked the white jerseys. They were a bit of a novelty. In the A-versus-B game the week before, we played in white jerseys to get used to it, with the other team in the amber and black that Down would be using. With any of those things, we tried as much as possible to make as little out of them as we could. At the end of the day, it's only a jersey and you can over-think things as well.

We stayed in Killiney the night before the game. It's a fairly relaxed spot anyway and you had no Cork or Down supporters there. We had our own team room with televisions and table-tennis and the physio, Colin Lane and the masseurs – Frank Cogan, another Cork legend, and Mick O'Leary.

These men were so important to the group from a physical perspective making sure our bodies were right, but also looking after your general well-being… they always offered great advice and always knew the right thing to say. Of course, Dr Con Murphy was always present, telling his fantastic stories and keeping everything light-hearted for the group in what was a high-pressure environment. Con is an amazing doctor and a great friend to all of us. He would do absolutely anything for anyone in our group.

The team room was where people congregated and had a bit of a laugh – they were always great weekends away with the team and the fact that it was a final didn't make things any different. It's funny how lads react on those weekends. Some lads love the banter and a bit of craic, others want to relax and go for walks and keep to themselves. Going to the Forty Foot for a swim was a big favourite for some of the lads. You can tell at meal-times that there's always a bit of nervousness but that's only natural, going into big occasions like that.

If you look at the first-half of that 2010 final, I don't think too many lads could hold their hands up and say that they played to their potential, but in the second-half, fellas really upped it. Ciarán, Paul Kerrigan, Donncha O'Connor, Walshie… all of these lads really took off and we did most of the damage in a 20-minute spell after half-time.

The introduction of Graham, who was carrying an injury, really settled the team. He was our leader and the energy of the crowd and team lifted when he came on. Then, Down came back into it, as you'd expect in a final, and in the last 10 minutes it was in the balance to an extent.

It's probably up there as one of my best performances. I scored eight of nine kicks from dead balls; there was one poor '45' in the first-half. In terms of being in the zone, it was one of those ones where myself and Donncha were kicking the ball well nearly every time and that's all you can ask for. There have been other days where I've been kicking frees and have put in the same amount of effort beforehand, and it doesn't happen for you. The year before, I kicked a few bad frees that were definitely a contributing factor to losing an All-Ireland final. It was great to see the flipside of it in 2010.

After that 2009 loss, I practised my frees throughout '10 with headphones in, playing crowd noise. If I didn't have them in, I was working on the mental side of it, more so than I would have done in the years previous. If you're not totally focused on what you're doing, then Croke Park is a different place to be taking frees. It can be daunting – if you don't have your mental routine set up, you're thinking about something else and, when you're in front of 40,000 or 50,000 people in a massive stadium, there are lots of things to be thinking about.

That's what I would have worked on, and I'd say Donncha would have been similar. We did a lot of work with our sports psychologist, Kevin Clancy on the mental side of it – Kevin is another great person and integral to the group. We really were blessed with the calibre of people involved in the backroom team and huge credit is due to Conor Counihan for the set-up, culture and environment that he created. Kicking the ball was never an issue but making sure that you were mentally set up to kick the ball correctly was the big thing.

I think our subs made a huge difference, steadying the ship. Graham, Nicholas Murphy, Derek Kavanagh, Colm O'Neill, Fintan Goold won a huge ball, John Hayes… all of these fellas had been around the block. We nearly worked on the premise of using four midfielders in 2009 and '10, and the final was no different; you needed the subs to close out the game. They had experience and that was the big thing about that panel, anyone could slot in and do a job on a given day.

That's why 30 lads go to Bere Island and do all the crap, and it's great for the starting 15 but it's hard for the other lads then. You've all the work done but you don't know if you're coming on, and you still have to be ready to do a job if you do. There was great credit due to the whole panel as it flip-flops – some years you're a starter, some years you're not. That was one of the special things about that group; there was never any hassle or giving out about guys not playing, and everyone understood that it was about the group rather than themselves.

After the game, I don't know was I that happy… it was more relief. The happiness came after but, at the final whistle, the relief was the over-riding thing for me. Looking back at it, the reaction from some lads was hilarious, running around Croke Park and sliding on the ground – for a group that didn't show our emotions too often, it was great to see fellas let loose!

We went back to the Burlington Hotel after the game and we had a great night. The next couple of days were mental; we went down to Bantry – Graham's club – on the Tuesday night and it was really enjoyable to spend time with all of the lads, having down-time and a few pints and just enjoying the experience. There was huge satisfaction at that point.

Under Conor Counihan, we won an All-Ireland, three Munster titles, three Division 1 league titles and one Division 2 title, but you'd often hear it thrown out that we should have won more. I would say that we could have won more as opposed to 'should have'. Unless something totally goes wrong – like a very strange refereeing decision, for example, which we never really had – the best team usually wins on a given day. We could have beaten Kerry in 2009, but that was one of the best Kerry teams of all time. We were playing very well in 2012 and we won Munster again, but Donegal had come with a new style and it was very hard to break them down. Maybe we might have won more, but you have to be happy with what you have, as well.

For our group, I think we got an awful lot out of it. You had some of the best players in the country, who had won little for the first 10 years of their careers but had crazy commitment to Cork football, and then you had the younger lads who had won under-21 All Irelands and come in new to the scene. What I remember is that, while it was absolutely unbelievable to get the Celtic Cross, the friendships that were born out of it was the biggest thing for me. I'm still great friends with nearly all of the panel.

I got to play with some great footballers and great men. I could go back and ask any one of them for help now and you'd get it straightaway. It really was and still is a special group and that enjoyed great success together.

MARK COLLINS

CORK 1-12 ★ KERRY 0-13 (AET)
Munster SFC Semi-Final
Páirc Uí Chaoimh
NOVEMBER 8, 2020

★ **CORK:** MA Martin; K O'Donovan (0-1), M Shanley, K Flahive; S Meehan, S Powter (0-1), M Taylor; I Maguire, P Walsh; J O'Rourke, K O'Hanlon (0-2), R Deane; **M Collins (0-4)**, C O'Callahan, B Hurley (0-1). **Subs:** M Keane (1-1) for O'Callaghan, L Connolly (0-2) for O'Rourke, M Hurley for Walsh, P Kerrigan for B Hurley, S White for O'Donovan, P Ring for Flahive, T Corkery for Powter, K O'Driscoll for Maguire, D Gore for O'Hanlon.

★ **KERRY:** S Ryan; J Foley, T Morley, T O'Sullivan; P Murphy, P Crowley, G White; D Moran, D O'Connor; B Ó Beaglaioch, S O'Shea (0-2), R Buckley (0-1); T Brosnan (0-1), D Clifford (0-4), D Moynihan (0-1). **Subs:** S O'Brien for Moynihan, K Spillane (0-4) for Brosnan, J Barry for Ó Beaglaioch, J Sherwood for Buckley, G Crowley for White, Ó Beaglaioch for O'Sullivan, T Walsh for Foley, P Clifford for O'Connor.

❝

THERE WERE SEVEN brothers in my father Francis' family and they all featured when Castlehaven played in the 1979 county SFC final. It was the club's first year up senior. My father and his brother Donal went to boarding school in Farranferris on the northside of Cork city, a real hurling nursery. My father would never have played any hurling before secondary school, but he loved it; he said it was one of the best things that ever happened to him. He made it on to the Cork panel – he came on as a sub in the 1982 and '83 All-Ireland final losses to Kilkenny. He also played one football league game for Cork.

Dad played club hurling for Blackrock, but I went to school in Douglas and played in their street leagues, so that's how I ended up playing hurling for them. Following family tradition, it was always going to be hard to say no to Castlehaven for football.

THE ACTION

★★★★★

THE COVID-19 PANDEMIC resulted in a winter championship and a return to straight knockout action, in front of an official attendance of zero. And yet, despite the unusual situation, this result had some similarities with 1983.

Once again, Cork managed to avoid going nine years without a win over Kerry; once again, they won it with a last-gasp goal at the city end – for Tadhg Murphy 37 years earlier, read sub Mark Keane, who was home from Australia, where he was playing in the AFL.

It was a cagey affair throughout. Kerry led four times in the opening 24 minutes, but three straight points, from Mark Collins, Killian O'Hanlon and Kevin O'Donovan meant Cork went in at half-time leading for the first time in the game.

The game remained close in the second-half, and both teams had their moments, before Kerry pushed on again in extra time. They led by two. The minute of injury time at the end of the second period of extra time was almost up as Cork held possession, with half-back Seán Meehan making a drive and exchanging passes with Damien Gore before laying off to Luke Connolly on the left.

He launched a high ball goalwards, but while it didn't go over the bar for an equaliser to send the game to penalties, possession was gathered by Keane and he slotted past Shane Ryan.

It was a first win over Kerry since 2012.

★★★★★

I was a dual Cork minor in 2008. In the football, we lost to Kerry by a point in the Munster semi-final in Páirc Uí Rinn. We had a good team but there was no second chance if you lost at the semi-final stage. We won the Munster minor hurling – we lost to Galway in the All-Ireland semi-final – but at the time, I was pretty much 50-50 between the two codes.

Something that probably had an effect was the fact that, back then, the under-21 football championship used to be early in the year, with the hurling later, and I got the call for the football panel in 2009, when I was just out of minor. I was probably a bit surprised at the time, but it turned out to be a great experience.

I was coming on as a sub all year, but then Shane McCarthy was sent off in the All-Ireland semi-final win over Dublin and I started the final against Down. It could have been daunting but I had been playing senior with Castlehaven for a couple of years by then. A good few of my minor team were involved that year – Ciarán Sheehan, Aidan Walsh, Paul Honohan, Liam Jennings, Darren Farry.

We had beaten Kerry well in Páirc Uí Rinn in our first game and then Tipperary in the Munster final, before Dublin in the All-Ireland semi – both games where we could have been beaten. We actually played fairly well but Down were winning near the end and we needed a Colm O'Driscoll goal right at the end to win.

I played under-21 hurling the following year, 2010, but I was poor. We lost to Tipperary; I was on Brendan Maher but I was taken off before half-time. By that stage, I had been called on to the senior football training panel, a 20-year-old playing A-versus-B games and the like. I was often marked by Ger Spillane and he was tough, the same with Noel O'Leary. You'd be wearing a bib and there weren't many times you'd come off with the bib intact! It was so physical, but it was some learning curve, though.

There was a great bond there and great craic; everybody seemed to get on and, of course, Cork won that All-Ireland. I was obviously outside the 'real' panel and Jim Nolan, who is from Castlehaven and was a selector, was asking if I wanted to go to the post-match banquet, but I didn't as I felt I was only on the fringes.

Earlier that year, the under-21 footballers had gone poorly, well beaten by Kerry in Tralee. In 2011, we walked through Munster – we hammered Kerry – but lost to Galway in the All-Ireland semi-final and that was a regret as they went on win the final well against Cavan. We didn't play at all against Galway – Paul Honohan had got injured after the Munster final and he was a big loss. It was definitely one that got away.

By that stage, I was on the football path with Cork – I had been called up to the full panel and it was just the way it had gone. I did get the call from Jimmy Barry-Murphy to go in for a couple of hurling practice matches in 2014 – the footballers had been knocked out by Mayo, the hurlers had won the Munster final, and I was asked in before the All-Ireland semi-final. It felt quite strange, a bit awkward, but you're not going to say no to JBM!

I made my senior championship debut with Cork against Down in a qualifier in 2011 as we had a rake of injuries – Ciarán Sheehan and Colm O'Neill were out, and then Daniel Goulding and Barry O'Driscoll got injured against Down. We won that match but lost to Mayo in the All-Ireland quarter-finals – the injuries were too much. It was disappointing, as the aim every year was to win the All-Ireland, but in 2012, we were flying again.

We won Munster and then played really well against Kildare in the All-Ireland quarter-finals. Before the semi against Donegal, there was a training camp at the Fota Island Resort and it was as well as I've ever seen that team going; they were absolutely hopping, but Donegal won by 0-16 to 1-11. I don't think Cork played badly that day... it could easily have gone the other way.

We missed a few chances before half-time and could have gone in three or four up, but when you were chasing that Donegal team, it was so tough. Donegal and Cork were probably the best two teams that year and it was as close as Cork came to winning it again. Over the next few years, the big characters from that team began dropping away and there were some frustrating results. The drawn game against Kerry in Killarney in 2015 was probably the biggest 'What if?'

Brian Cuthbert had come in as manager in 2014, after Conor Counihan left, and obviously changed a lot. For 2015, he brought in Pat Flanagan for strength and conditioning and the training we put in that year was absolutely crazy. I kept a diary at the time and we were doing something most days of the week – in January, we only missed a couple of days!

We were really going well, and we came so close to beating Kerry – they got a goal from a controversial penalty and then a last-minute equaliser. We lost to them in the replay, and we were knocked out of the championship a week later in the qualifiers against Kildare. There was a decent team there and if we had won Munster there would have been something to build on, but 'Cubby' left and we lost more players and had some tough years. The continuity was never there – inter-county management is a tough job and there's such a steep learning curve, with strength and conditioning and everything. There was so much change, you were building on quicksand.

For most of my Cork career, I was a forward, usually the half-forward line, but I played sweeper at times in 2015 and it wasn't something you took much notice of. You buy into absolutely everything and, no matter what year, you felt that you were going well. I loved that year – when I'd go back down to West Cork, people would ask what I was doing back there, but I found it enjoyable and I was able to get forward too as I got on loads of ball.

The next three years were disappointing but there were some signs of growth again in 2019. We only lost to Kerry by three points, having been beaten by them by 17 points in 2018, and we went on and reached the Super 8s, the All-Ireland quarter-final round-robin. I felt that we got very close as a group. We had two training camps in Dublin that summer – we used to use Kilmacud Crokes' grounds for our training and we were staying in Ballsbridge – and there were two games in Croke Park, against Tyrone and Dublin. So you had four trips up there, staying in the same hotel, lads really bonded. I used to room with Luke Connolly and I got on super with him.

Then, Covid hit in 2020. Cork had won the under-20 All-Ireland in 2019, but those lads missed the chance to come in properly into the senior set-up. Again, that bit of continuity was gone. In saying that, the first lockdown went quite well – Kevin Smith was the strength and conditioning coach, he had come in with Cian O'Neill, and we had a lot of contact with each other on Zoom and in WhatsApp groups.

We were all given GPS units and all of our sessions were tracked. We trained hard. I'm living in Grange and so I used to go over to Tramore Valley Park or the steep hill at Vernon Mount – the same place where my father used to train with Larry Tompkins in the 1980s. Mentally, it was very good and I enjoyed it.

Then, when we were able to get back in small pods, five or six of us used to go to the Farm in Bishopstown, which is owned by UCC. I was with Brian and Michael Hurley, Seán Powter and Ian Maguire. We had a good gang and it was enjoyable.

When GAA returned, the club championships were played first and Castlehaven had a good year. We made it to the county semi-final and beat St Finbarr's in a penalty shootout after an epic game on October 4, but the following day all GAA activity was suspended and the county final against Nemo Rangers wouldn't be played until the following August.

It was a very strange scenario. We had picked up a few knocks in the Barrs game and we were like the walking wounded coming out of Páirc Uí Rinn that night. When the final was postponed, we were almost relieved, as we felt we hadn't a ghost of a chance if it was played the following week.

Cork had played five league games before the lockdown, winning all of them. We were down in Division 3 that year and were expected to get promoted but there was a lot of confidence taken from them. When inter-county started again, we beat Louth to secure promotion and we were due to play Longford in the final round but we were given a walkover as they couldn't field. At the time, that was seen as a blow as it denied us a warm-up for the Munster semi-final against Kerry.

Those of us whose clubs had long championship campaigns were back later with Cork. I remember driving in for training the first night I was back and thinking, This is mad, as things were very strict at the time, but it was a real bonus to have it when everybody else was locked down. Once you're back with the group, it's like things are back to normal all of a sudden.

For the Louth match, you didn't take much notice of the lack of a crowd, as league matches in Páirc Uí Chaoimh are normally that way anyway. The day of the Kerry game, it definitely felt like a weird situation.

We met at Rochestown Park Hotel. Aidan Kelleher was the team doctor and he was very good to ensure that all of the guidelines were met. For team meetings, you had all of the windows open... you were allowed 15 minutes, and then you had to go outside for a five-minute walk. It was November too, so trying to do anything outside was nearly impossible.

I was named corner-forward and I had Tom O'Sullivan marking me. I wasn't at all sure that I'd be starting; it was really touch and go because I had missed the whole league before the lockdown. Then I got injured against the Barrs in the county semi-final – a lump on my back that I had to have drained – and, up to the morning of the Louth game, they weren't sure if I'd be able to play any bit.

I came on against Louth and, to be honest, I didn't think I'd be starting against Kerry because I had very little done with Cian and that group. I kind of copped it during the week then, with the way that we were setting up in training and that, that it was likely that I would be.

Kerry had only lost the 2019 All-Ireland final after a replay and we were obviously underdogs, but that didn't really matter. No matter what match we played over the years, we always thought that we were going well and that we were in with a right chance. I became very good friends with Ian Maguire and we used to have a routine where we'd have a coffee the morning of a match, before going to meet the bus. I picked him up before the Kerry match in Killarney in 2017 and we were full certain we'd win… but then afterwards we were wondering if we were deluded.

At the same time, you had to keep believing. In 2019 in the Páirc, we hadn't been given a chance, but we only lost by three points. It was a great game and the supporters really got behind us. We built on that then in the qualifiers.

For the 2020 game, I was on the frees. I was taking them for Castlehaven at the time – I'd have always taken them underage for Castlehaven, but then Brian Hurley took over. When Brian got injured with his hamstrings, I started taking them again.

I wouldn't be a massive man to take too many in the warm-up, but I'd always like to finish on a score. I've always had the same routine – the way I'd hold the ball and how many looks I'd take at the goal. I got into taking them for Castlehaven in around 2008. Brendan Deasy was taking the left-footed frees at the time – he was living in Carrigaline, only five minutes from me, so we used to go to Ballygarvan and practice. We got obsessed … we used to go there twice a week if we could, and it grew from there. As time went on, I wouldn't do as much practice. I suppose, once you get into your routine, it's not as essential.

To be fair to Ronan McCarthy, he was a massive believer that there was talent in that team. He was fully convinced that the team was good enough to go all the way. He thought that was in that panel and that probably went through the team, then. In 2019, there had been a lot of positives – I know everybody went on about the challenge matches and how well they went, but I think they definitely gave the group a bit of self-belief that was needed. We beat some good teams and, even though the Super 8s didn't go our way, some of the performances were good.

When the opportunity came against Kerry, the self-belief was there, especially as the game went on… and we stayed with them. It grew in lads, and that meant that we were able to take the opportunity.

Cian O'Neill was big on trying to stop Tom O'Sullivan, Gavin White and Paul Murphy – the two wing-backs and the corner-back. Obviously, they do a lot of damage, so myself, Ruairí Deane and John O'Rourke were nearly doing marking jobs when Kerry had the ball. I found myself back very deep at times and that helped me pick up some loose ball.

It was a close game all the way through, but Kerry were managing to stay in front. Then, near the end, we were a point down and won a free… it was an edge-of-the-D job. Over the years, sometimes you'd be very nervous but, whatever way that match went, things just seemed to flow and it was just another kick.

I suppose I was lucky that I had taken a few with Castlehaven that year and so you're used to it. I found that, the older I got and the more experienced I got, they got easier, just from putting myself in that position so often over the years – I know people often say the opposite in sports like golf. I remember taking them in 2009 with Castlehaven and I missed two very bad ones against the Barrs, but I found that it was a learning curve as I went on and I got more used to taking them. Thankfully, the ball went over and the game went to extra time.

There were no dressing-rooms or anything, so we were still out on the pitch. With us having got the leveller, the feeling coming in for the team talk was massive. Ronan's speech was just about going on and winning it… there was nothing said about opportunities gone or anything.

It was the same in extra time, but again Kerry nudged in front and they had a one-point lead again with time almost up. We had done a lot of work on being patient and we recycled and recycled, before Luke Connolly sent a kick goalwards. Ronan did a bit of analysis on it afterwards; he asked us if Luke was right to go for it and the decision was that he was, we were probably going nowhere with it and he was our best kicker.

There wasn't enough on the kick to go over the bar, but Mark Keane was there to win it and slot it home. The elation was unbelievable.

Mark had spent very little time with the group. He was in maybe a week and a half or two weeks before the Kerry game, but he was really impressive in training. His handling was unreal. That was one thing I really noticed – no matter what way the ball was kicked into him, it stuck. That showed with the goal he got.

There were no celebrations afterwards as we couldn't go anywhere but we drove out that day and there were supporters lined up to cheer us – that was as good a feeling as you'd ever have after a match. There were little kids there with flags and it was a crazy situation. Normally, you might meet your parents or family afterwards, but obviously none of them were there and you were ringing them. It was weird, but it was class.

Unfortunately, we lost to Tipperary in the Munster final. Because we didn't go on to beat Tipp, the shine is taken off the memory of the Kerry match a small bit, to be honest. I think the elation of the Kerry game and the buzz, it was very hard to come back down from. It was one we had waited for, for a long time and there were a lot of players who had suffered disappointment against Kerry and I don't think we ever really truly came back down off it.

There was a two-week gap between the games. We trained the following Saturday, an A v B game, and we were brutal. Tipp weren't a bad team – we had a good few battles with them over the years and they didn't fear us at all. We were just as flat as pancakes and it definitely does take away something because all the talk is now that we caught Kerry on the hop and it was a one-off miracle. If you'd beaten Tipp, you were in an All-Ireland semi-final against Mayo, and I think that that Cork team would have had a right crack off them.

It was a great opportunity and who knows what could have happened. Just the way we played, we were so poor.

I retired from inter-county football after 2021, when Kerry beat us in the Munster final. It was something that I had been thinking about for a while, as it's such a big commitment. I had been involved with Cork since I was 14.

In 2022, I went on a summer holiday and that was the first time I'd been able to do it since back then. I absolutely love Cork and it was so hard to make the call. Keith Ricken came in as manager after Ronan, and I had him when I was under-15; obviously John Cleary, the coach then and manager now, is Castlehaven and I had played with selector James Loughrey, become very good friends with him and been at his wedding.

That made it even harder, feeling that I was letting them down, but it was a decision I had to make for myself. I went to nearly every match – the Kerry game in Páirc Uí Rinn in 2022, I don't think I ever supported a team so much. I was kicking every ball, but at the same time I didn't feel that I should have been out there. I knew it was the right call then.

IAN MAGUIRE

CORK 1-14 ★ ROSCOMMON O-16
All-Ireland SFC Preliminary Quarter-Final
Páirc Uí Chaoimh
JUNE 24, 2023

★ **CORK:** MA Martin; T Walsh (0-1), D O'Mahony, M Shanley; L Fahy (0-1), R Maguire (0-2), M Taylor (0-1); C O'Callaghan, **I Maguire**; K O'Hanlon, S Powter, B O'Driscoll (0-1); R Deane, S Sherlock (0-5), E McSweeney. **Subs:** C Óg Jones (0-2) for McSweeney, C Corbett (1-0) for Deane, K O'Donovan (0-1) for Shanley, T Clancy for Fahy, J O'Rourke for O'Hanlon.

★ **ROSCOMMON:** C Carroll (0-1; D Murray, B Stack, N Daly; C Hussey, C Daly, E McCormack; E Nolan, D Ruane; C Murtagh (0-5), E Smith (0-2), C McKeon; D Smith, B O'Carroll, D Murtagh (0-6). **Subs:** C Cox for Smith, D Cregg (0-2) for Ruane, K Doyle for Nolan, C Connolly for Hussey, R Hughes for N Daly.

"

GROWING UP IN Togher, it felt like everybody played soccer and GAA– you just played with St Finbarr's, and either Greenwood or Everton, that was it.

I grew up only a few minutes' walk from the Barrs and we just spent so much time there. There was no rugby outlet or anything else, and that's still the way. I'd have been friends with a lot of fellas that still play soccer and we'd play astro over the winter. I don't know if I knew that I had the potential to play football for Cork. It was just a case that you liked it and cared a lot about it. We were always there or thereabouts as a team, and then the group would all have been best friends, so all we did was play with the Barrs or play with Greenwood.

I started playing minor for the Barrs when I was 16, and we won a county and it went on from there. I played hurling and football but, even though I did play senior hurling for a few years, I was always better at football and our age-group

THE ACTION

★★★★★

IN THE FIRST year of the new round-robin format for the All-Ireland series, the Rebels had come with a stirring comeback to beat Mayo the previous week and take second place in their group behind Mayo; this win meant that it was the first time Cork had beaten two Division 1 sides in the same championship since 2009.

The opening stages saw Roscommon dictate matters, with Ciaráin Murtagh scoring four points, and his brother Diarmuid two, as the Connacht side moved into a 0-7 to 0-3 lead. They had rallied to trail by just one at half-time, though, and Rory Maguire levelled the match at 0-7 each immediately after action resumed.

Steven Sherlock, Luke Fahy and a Sherlock's free made it 0-12 to 0-10, before Roscommon sub Daire Cregg pulled one back after a mark. But Cork struck for their goal after sub Conor Corbett linked with Seán Powter, and his shot trickled in off the post.

When Jones added another, it was a five-point game but Roscommon diligently ate into the lead. Ciaráin Murtagh's fifth point of the day had the sides level as injury time dawned and, when Davy Burke's side claimed possession, they seemed primed to work a scoring opportunity.

Cork forced a turnover, though. Seán Powter drove forward and Ian Maguire's run created space. Rather than taking his own score, Maguire found sub Kevin O'Donovan and he fisted over for what was the winning score.

★★★★★

had better results in football. With Greenwood, we got to the quarter-finals of the national cup one year – we lost to Knock from Mayo. We had beaten a star-studded Corinthian Boys team along the way, even though they were a division above us – we robbed them blind, really! They had Brian Lenihan, who went on to play for Cork City and Hull City, Rob Lehane, who also played for Cork City, Micheál Martin, my Cork teammate now, and Jamie Davis, who I would also have played with at under-age.

My father John is from Glasheen – his own father is from Ballydehob – and he'd never have played GAA at all. My two uncles played a small bit, but nothing major. My old man was a boxer. I never tried it and he always hangs it over me, 'It's easy in a team sport… you were never in there on your own!' On my mother, Marian's side, there would be more of a soccer and GAA background, though it'd be more Lough Rovers and Ballyphehane.

I only played one year at minor level for Cork. My age was one of the last before the Rebel Óg development squads came in. There were regional teams – I played for the city side, Seandún, under Keith Ricken and Tony Davis – and I went for trials for my under-17 year, 2011, but I was useless so I had no complaints.

When I did make the team for my last year minor, we lost to Tipperary in the Munster semi-final in Páirc Uí Chaoimh. We bottled it, really, there's no two ways about it.

One consolation was that the Barrs won the minor county in 2012 and I went in to UCC, where I would have been playing Freshers football. Then I got a call to go in for a couple of under-21 challenge games – John Cleary was the manager at the time – and you're delighted to be playing in those matches. I remember coming on in one of them, I think it was against Roscommon, and I did alright and then the next thing I'm named to start in the Munster quarter-final against Kerry.

I was kind of surprised because someone like Jamie Davis wasn't picked to start, even though he was on the age and he was better than me. It was a bit controversial – and Jamie was giving me a lift to training too and he's sound! John and the selectors obviously just made the call and I kept the position then.

We beat Kerry in the first match, and then we got on a bit of a run and went all the way to the All-Ireland final but we lost to Galway. The Barrs were knocked out in the fourth round of the championship in 2013, so I wasn't playing anything in the latter part of the year, but then playing for UCC was a big help. Being honest, it was one of the main reasons that I played for Cork, as it helped me to kick on.

Billy Morgan was the manager and I was playing midfield alongside David Nation from Nemo. I got to mark Michael Darragh Macauley, James Walsh from Kerry, who was seen as a rising star, Niall McKeever from Antrim, who went on to play Australian Rules football, and Mattie Donnelly. I did alright against them, and we won the Sigerson Cup.

What I probably wouldn't have fully appreciated beforehand was that the age gap in the Sigerson is frightening. Even at under-21, there could be a two-year difference, but I was up against guys who were 23 or 24... and I was only 19, about to turn 20. That stands to you.

I went from that to another good year with the under-21s – we lost to Roscommon in the All-Ireland semi-final, an infamous game where they got away with a ball picked up off the floor – and then I was brought into the senior panel. I was training away and in the A-versus-B games I used to play half-back, marking Mark Collins and John O'Rourke, because there were a lot of good midfielders there at the time. There was Aidan Walsh, Fintan Goold, Ruairí Deane and Seán Dineen... so I was fifth or sixth or whatever. Then I ended up starting against Sligo and Mayo in the championship!

When I came on to the senior panel, I went flat-out with the gym work and that helped me to develop. Though then I hurt my back lifting, so I obviously wasn't that great at it! After our second league game, a win up in Monaghan, I was throwing my bag in the boot of the bus and I felt a huge pain in my back. It was very sore all the way back and I didn't think anything of it. When we got home, I called to see Stephen Goggin, one of my best friends, and we were chatting about the game in his kitchen and I was saying that my back was killing me. I went to bed, still expecting it would go away... and I didn't play for another seven months.

I made the bench for the Kildare game, when Cork got knocked out of the championship. Soon after that, the Barrs were playing Brian Dillons in the city junior championship and I was eligible. I ended up breaking my ankle and I was gone for another few months. It was some run!

I went from playing constantly to not playing at all, but I learned a lot from it. What I found hard was the fact that it was just me doing the work with the Cork physio, Colin Lane for company while the team were training. Now, rehab is done more in a group, maybe because there are more injuries. It was like that for five months and I always felt like I was making progress, and then something would happen and I'd be knocked back. It was like constantly having the chair pulled out from under me.

I can remember around the time of the 2015 Munster final replay, I felt like I was nearly there in terms of getting back on the panel… and I suffered a reoccurrence. I got an epidural but I was thinking that I'd never play again – you just have these thoughts in your head, that you won't get back to the level for inter-county and would just have to play with the club and be careful with the back.

Colin and I had an argument one day when we were starting rehab again. It was a simple drill where he'd roll the ball to me and I'd pick it up and give him a handpass, but I was saying that I didn't want to do it as I didn't feel I was ready. 'I'll do the straight-line running but I can't do this,' I said, and Colin absolutely ripped me asunder – borderline tears. Sometimes you just need a bollocking to get out of your own head. Thankfully, I recovered and that injury hasn't affected me since.

In 2013 and '14, I played senior for the Barrs in football and hurling. I started the relegation final against Ballinhassig in 2013. Then I hurt my back in 2015, so I didn't play. I came back in 2016 and played intermediate for a couple of years but didn't really play at all after that. In 2016, Cork lost to Donegal in the All-Ireland qualifiers on a Sunday and, two days later, I togged out for the intermediate hurlers against Ballygarvan. I was on the bench and came on for the last 10 minutes. It was a draw and we beat them in a replay.

Brian Cuthbert stood down as Cork manager at the end of 2015, and Peadar Healy took over. In 2016, maybe you had the hangover of an old management into a new management, and there was a big turnover in players. A lot of more established players were injured and then new players came in. In 2017, I was dropped during the league so I wasn't thrilled with how that year went! Alan O'Connor had come back – which was good for Cork as he was a superb player – and I was sub for the first round of Munster against Waterford.

We had only beaten Waterford by a point – when you're low on confidence and you get rattled, it's very hard to shake it off. Alan was sent off and I came in for the Tipperary match.

Paul Kerrigan had been the captain, but he missed a lot of the league in 2018 as Nemo Rangers got to the All-Ireland club final. Ronan McCarthy, who had taken over from Peadar, made me vice-captain... so I was captain a lot during the spring. I had captained a lot of underage teams in the Barrs, and I was UCC captain in 2017, the same year as I became the senior skipper for the Barrs.

I think I'm an okay communicator and that is an element of leadership. I suppose I was always a bit vocal on the pitch when I was younger; I used to say what I thought, whether that might be right or wrong, and that probably played a part too. There's leading by example, too – in the Barrs, Colin 'House' Lyons is a tremendous leader but you're not getting two words out of him! Just the way he plays, it gives leadership – the same with Michael Shields. They front up and I would have taken a leaf out of their book.

Ronan probably learned an awful lot in 2018. He was doing a lot himself and there was still a big turnover in players, and strength and conditioning coaches. Adam Doyle, who is a great S&C coach, was in his first year too.

We got our arses handed to us by Kerry, and then Tyrone, two teams who were way ahead of us all across the board. In 2019, Eddie Kirwan came in as coach, Ronan took a step back and there was huge development there. It was year two with Adam as S&C coach and, if you ever needed any evidence of how benefits come over time, the likes of Matty Taylor and Killian O'Hanlon had become serious inter-county operators. We were close, but we never got the big win that have really pushed us over the edge.

The Tyrone Super 8s game in Croke Park is probably the best example. If we had won that match, it would have really propelled us forward. To make real progress, you need to proceed in the competition. After we lost to Tyrone and Dublin, we had Roscommon at home in the last match, both of us having lost twice and that was probably a damning indication of the mentality of the group, to be honest. If we had won that, it would have been a boost, but we didn't and the reaction was kind of like, 'Same old Cork'.

Midfield or centre-back was almost always where I played. When I played minor for Cork, Ephie Fitzgerald did play me centre-forward a couple of times because we had a lot of big guys around midfield – Cillian O'Connor from Mallow, Alan O'Donovan from Nemo, Paul Fitzgerald from Douglas.

I remember coming from underage to senior and having to mark Séamie O'Shea, and realising it was a totally different beast. You go from being the strongest at your own age to the weakest at senior, so there are learnings there; and then just things like kickouts, positioning and so on. Aidan Walsh was there in 2014 and then he was gone in '15, but Fintan Goold and Andrew O'Sullivan were still there so you're learning your trade off these guys.

In transitioning from then all the way to now, different players would have put their hands up in midfield. I would probably have the best relationship with Killian O'Hanlon because we've played together so long, since under-21, and we're friends. Killian has been very unlucky with injuries; he has had long stints out but managed to come back. Paul Walsh made a strong claim and played some championship games, but then Colm O'Callaghan came on strongly over the last two years. Paul is still there and challenging, so it's a good midfield developing and you'd hope that that can be powered forward.

I can remember going into the Kerry game in 2020 thinking that I wasn't ready. It was after the county championship and we had had devastating loss to Castlehaven in the semi-finals. It was the worst loss I've ever had – beaten on penalties by a team that we would have thought that we were better than at that time.

The Kerry game felt totally independent from everything else that was going on in the world at the time. You were playing your neighbours, the team that you most want to beat, in a one-off game. To get that win was huge, but it was ultimately linked to a major disappointment as we lost the Munster final to Tipperary. At the time, it was gutting but, looking back, it probably helped to make me the player I am now.

It was a massive missed opportunity and I was captain at the time so something like that falls at your doorstep. You can't let it define you though, and what you can do is use it as a reference and say that it won't be allowed to happen again.

Against Kerry in Killarney in 2021, that was a game where we were outplayed and outrun. You can break it down into tactics or whatever, but I don't think that we as individuals prepared for that year overall and the proof was in the pudding at the end. If I ask myself now, was I ready to play at a high level against Kerry, no would the answer and I think a lot of other fellas would say the same. We went up by 1-5 to 0-3 in the first-half – that showed the promise, but the rest of the game showed the reality and there was a huge difference between the two.

The Barrs won the county in 2021 and we went on to win the Munster Club Championship against Austin Stacks and reached the All-Ireland semi-final – we lost to Kilcoo after extra time. Myself and the other Barrs lads missed the first two league games, against Roscommon and Clare, but we were back the week after the Kilcoo game.

Not long after that, we played Clare in a challenge match in Mallow. Conor Jordan, who plays for Austin Stacks, had joined Clare and we were having words as it wasn't long after the Munster final. He got a hand-pass and I went for a challenge, but I hit his elbow with my hand – down to Mallow General Hospital for myself to see a big break in my hand! I was out for four weeks and, when I came back, I put padding on my hand and goalkeeper gloves over it… I had them from when I broke the other hand a year previously. With glass hands like that, you can see why I didn't follow my dad into the boxing!

Keith Ricken had taken over from Ronan as manager for 2022. With a new management coming in, there was probably a bit of inexperience and we were a bit behind at the start of the year, and lost our first few league games. Then Keith had to step away for health reasons and John Cleary stepped up from coach to manager. By that stage, we were battling against relegation from Division 2 and that was extra important from 2022 onwards, as the Tailteann Cup was being introduced for the 16 lowest-ranked teams. We had two league games left, against Down and Offaly, and we basically had to win both of them to retain our Sam Maguire status.

While I was away with the Barrs, Keith had made Brian Hurley and Seán Meehan joint-captains. I didn't view it as a demotion or anything, to be fair. I'm best friends with Brian, so there's no issue there, and Seán is a natural leader, probably one of the fellas you'd be saying was next in line. I wasn't going to give any less just because I wasn't captain.

Every game we played under John was like a building block in terms of fitness and football – Adam Doyle was back in as S&C coach too, which helped. We always felt like we were making a gradual progression, albeit coming from a low base – they're the facts, if you're in Division 2, it means you're under-performing.

When it came to the championship, we were kind a of 60- or 65-minute team and then trying to hold on at the end, but we showed good promise. People said we got a handy draw in beating Limerick and Louth to get to an All-Ireland quarter-final, but fast-forward 12 months and nobody was wanting to draw Louth.

We were outclassed by Dublin and that showed up a lot of small things, but I think there was a lot of potential shown. There was a kind of a reality check when John became manager as we were in a tough spot but I think that we ultimately rallied around ourselves and the management, which created a good foundation for 2023. John then got Kevin Walsh involved and we went from strength to strength then based off that.

Inter-county is now so team-based. Not that club is just a collection of individuals, but inter-county has such a team-orientation that there is probably a transition when you come back. I think people are coming around to that now, whereas before, people saw someone kick five points for their club and expected the same for Cork, but you might have had to evolve into a ball-winning forward at inter-county rather than being a pure out-and-out scorer.

I've had a couple of coaches over the last few years and you learn different things from them. With Cian O'Neill, who was in under Ronan McCarthy, I'd have learned a lot of individual things to improve my own game – I think I did, anyway! In 2023, Kevin Walsh implemented a lot of new things, or at least a polished version of things that we had been doing, around defensive systems and kickout structures. At the start of the year, I wouldn't have been able to identify all the things that we went on to learn. He has an excellent demeanour about him and he has been very good to us.

Obviously, we improved defensively and I think that our kickouts went from strength to strength. There's no big magical 'tactic' but he built on a lot of the basics in training and then you're taking that into matches. We had a lot of setbacks as well during the year, but we were able to improve overall and I think we showed that.

When I came in first, midfield play was probably transitioning. It was pretty much 45-to-45 but then the likes of Aidan Walsh and Michael Dara Macauley began evolving it to something where it became box-to-box. At the time I began, you had the likes of Aidan O'Shea, Séamie O'Shea, Neil Gallagher and Alan

O'Connor, but you also had Aidan and Macauley too, so it was kind of chalk and cheese in a way, even though Séamie O'Shea was probably a version of both.

By now, it has progressed more and more… and more, to where it's almost like a hybrid half-back – someone like James McCarthy, who was traditionally a right half-back, is just as effective a midfielder now. Brian Fenton, you could play him right half-back or right half-forward just as easily as midfield, because he has all the attributes. David Moran was almost a throwback but he still had the mobility and his footballing was at such a high level. Athleticism, box-to-box and scoring have become really important key performance indicators for a midfielder now.

The difference in tackling is something that I find very interesting between club and inter-county level. At club, I always feel that you get punished if there's a show of strength in the tackle. If you're caught in the tackle at club level, it's almost always a free, whereas at inter-county it's a turnover. To be fair, the referees in Cork are getting better and they are focusing in on technique and I do have sympathy for them as it is tricky.

We won the McGrath Cup at the start of 2023 and we were obviously hoping to get promotion from Division 2 of the league, but we were well beaten by Meath in our opening match. I think that the Meath and Clare game have similarities in that they were each the start of a new competition, coming after a block of work – and a set of expectations, to be honest.

People can talk about a lack of effort and whether you're fit enough or fast enough or good enough. That game is an example of things going against us – which is normal – but when things turned, we made it way worse for ourselves rather than Clare making it way worse for us. The fact we only got a few points from play was obviously heavily reported but shooting-wise, we really let ourselves down and gave away a lot of turnovers. Kickout-wise, were we getting in the right positions for breaks and getting beaten.

That was always going to be a three-point game – it was windy, it was cold and it was in Ennis against a good Clare team. We didn't show enough maturity to see out a game where we four points ahead.

I watch a lot of GAA and my friends and I would always go to county championship matches. Though, after the Barrs or Cork get knocked out I tend not to watch, so

I've never been to a county senior football final that I haven't played in and I've been to All-Ireland hurling finals supporting Cork but not a football one.

Similarly, the 2023 Munster football final wasn't on my radar after Clare beat us but at least we had the new round-robin to focus on. It's hard to compare the value of six weeks' preparation against the value of getting a championship game. You can't win enough, especially championship games with a young team. The attitude that we took after Clare was that we were going to use our time well. Ultimately, what kick-started the second part of the championship season was that there was an internal discussion along the lines of, 'We did all this work – why did we not do X and Y?' We felt we had to front up and face the facts and, if those facts were lack of ability and tactics or whatever, we had to address them and move on.

It was back to the drawing board then in terms of how we were training, building on that and maybe getting two or three percent fitter and nailing how we wanted to play. That's what the six weeks were about, though ultimately, it still comes down to beating Louth by two points. You have to win games to show that what you're doing is right and to compete. There's a certain level of uncontrollable in a game, where you have to show your worth.

There were positives and negatives in having Louth first. Number one, they're perceived as the weakest team of the three but the negative is that you're playing a type of football that we're not the strongest in the country at. You're playing against 15 defenders and trying to move the ball and then facing counter-attacks. When we played Mayo, maybe the game was bit more open – and it wasn't all that open – but the Louth match was cagey and closeted. The fact that we had played them in the league definitely helped.

I think the Kerry game was, outside of the Derry match, ultimately the most disappointing, in the sense that it was there for us and we just never really pushed on. It wasn't a lack of effort or a lack of ability – or maybe that to a certain extent – but it was that we made key mistakes at crucial junctures. That's what drove us into the Mayo game; the feeling that we misfired rather than consoling ourselves that we were there or thereabouts. It was an important narrative to have within the group and we went to Limerick thinking we were there to top the group rather than keep the score low or navigate a one-point win.

The biggest learning from all the games up to the Mayo match was that we encountered bad moments, like conceding a goal, but didn't compound them with more errors. It's very simple terminology but when Mayo scored their goal, we got a quick kickout and drove up the field, drove at the opposition. In those situations, the biggest thing is that you don't allow a turnover and don't do anything crazy.

We got the ball to Colm O'Callaghan, who's a strong runner, and he drove at the defence and we won a penalty. It could have been a free in – or a free out! – but the theory is that you do what you're comfortable doing: long kickout, get the ball to a runner and create an opportunity. We went from a bad error to good play from Cork and, regardless of whether we got a goal or not, we mentally learned not to compound something.

That was the fundamental change in that game – we showed maturity after a bad juncture. A lot of games are tight now, only one or two scores in them, so if you lose a big moment, you have to manage the game after that. We showed our fitness levels and our tactical nuance in terms of how we managed the game. I think, ultimately, we showed our ability and it all came together that day.

The way the structure is now, if you get out of your group you're going to be playing a good team – there's no soft backdoor game. We had played Roscommon in a challenge game so automatically you've some bit of familiarity. When you get a big win, it just reaffirms what you're doing so there was a good bit of confidence going into the Roscommon game. We had a big opportunity to win a championship game at home and that was how we painted it, regardless of who we were playing.

I have two different pre-match rituals that have developed. With the Barrs, we'd play cards – Poker or Take Two – but the night before a Cork game, I play Xbox at home, *Call of Duty or Battlefield*. People are blown away by that but it's just what I do! I play away, online against other people, and I go to bed; it's a way of separating myself from the match and not thinking about it.

We meet at Cork Airport Hotel for home games – they do a great chicken stir-fry! We'd usually have a quick chat after the meal and get the bus down with the tunes on and straight into the dressing-room. When John Cooper was on the panel, he had a big toolbox-style DeWalt speaker but he's gone to America now so we had to get another one. There's a good mix of songs – it's a group playlist so fellas can put on whatever they want.

With the Barrs, I had always worn the No 8 jersey and it was the same for Cork under Ronan. I came back at the start of 2023 after a disappointing county final loss with the Barrs and feeling that I had a point to prove. Colm was flying in midfield and I almost took it that he was the number-one midfielder and I was chasing him, even though we were playing together. I was given the 9 jersey early on in the year and I was using it as subtle motivation, purely created in my own head.

I'd always have an idea of who I'm marking – what leg, have you played him before, strengths and weaknesses. Before we played Mayo, I had my homework done on Matthew Ruane and Diarmuid O'Connor; I ended up picking up Ruane. I knew if he got on the ball, it was important not to give him a head-start because he'd look for a one-two.

You learn a lot as you go, and then you have our own visualisation in terms of what you want to do. I'd always play out different scenarios – the inclination is to stick to the positive ones but you try to develop situations where you're defending, within reason.

I know Enda Smith of Roscommon like the back of my hand, as he's the same age as me and I've played against him all the way up. I know he has no left leg so you try to get him on to that side… but then he kicked a point against Cork with the outside of his right foot! I never thought he'd take the shot on but it just goes to show you can't prepare for everything.

It took a while for that game to get going. I looked at the clock and saw that there were 20 minutes gone, which I couldn't believe because it was so flat and so dead. We knew what to expect in terms of how they played – there's a certain element of soccer to it, with a lot of off-the-ball movement and long periods of possession. It was new territory to a degree as we had never played a team like that. Even against Louth, when they get the ball, they're still trying to beat you quickly, rather than death by a thousand cuts like Roscommon.

In the game, it was about getting comfortable and then, as it went on, having more and more belief. We started pushing up on their kickouts and generating a bit of momentum. In the second-half, Conor Corbett and Chris Óg Jones came on, so we had a bit of firepower but Roscommon had one great goal chance. Thankfully, Micheál Martin made a brilliant save and there was a huge feeling of relief.

When we got the goal and had a bit of a lead, we had all the momentum but, to be fair, Roscommon are an experienced team and they kept tipping away at us. In the modern game, subs make such a big impact and that's what happened. Both Roscommon midfielders went off and traditionally you'd be delighted with that but now you're thinking, *Oh no, this fella is fresh as a daisy.*

One of the big things is to keep doing what you're doing, no matter what. People talked about me passing to Kevin O'Donovan for the winning point as if it was the first time it ever happened, but I must have made that run a hundred times this year. We were obviously very tired but, the minute the ball turned over, I remember thinking, *Get into position.* When I got into position, I knew straightaway I was on... and I was screaming at Seán Powter to give it to me.

He didn't actually give it to me the first time, but he did the second time. What I only know best is take the ball at pace and beat the man. I bounced the ball and went between two people and then I saw Kevin. I could have popped it over myself but I play the same way I have for 15 years – people give out, but I always look for the pass. To be fair, he slotted it over straightaway.

When you're playing at the level, you're ultimately there for what you do best and you have to trust in that, and then develop other parts of your game. I was shouting at Powter because I knew I could split the gap and lay it off. The game started with me doing that and setting up Sherlock for a point and the game ended with me doing it.

Against Derry in the All-Ireland quarter-final, we wasted a lot of chances early in the game. In that environment, we definitely struggled to shoot under pressure and that handicapped us. The other thing was that we didn't stick exactly to what we were supposed to do later in the game. Against Mayo and Roscommon, we followed up scoring a goal by overturning their kickout and getting a point, but Derry secured their kickout after our goal.

That in itself probably made us panic a small bit and then our overload became a one-on-one kickout for them, and they got a goal. Something that had worked well for us twice didn't work a third time – was that because it was better opposition or was it a different environment? It was disappointing because it was there for us and we kept a lot of their big players quiet.

They managed the game well. The final scoreline might show a margin but our shooting efficiency was disappointing. Myself, I had two shots and two misses and you should be at least taking one of those two. Everybody was probably individually thinking they didn't play up to scratch but there was probably a collective element of not managing the game.

We're looking to 2024 with a lot of continuity in terms of players and management. We'll be in year two with Kevin Walsh and building on the S&C gains we made this year rather than playing catch-up. Physically, we can be top two or top three athleticism-wise and then build your skills into that and carry in the form from 2023.

Your ambition should be an All-Ireland, it always should be, especially if you're from Cork. No matter how good or bad the situation is, that should be the aim.

Printed in Great Britain
by Amazon

40166785R00118